DATE DUE

AG 6 '33			
JY 21 '94			
JE 1 '95			
DO 21 '99			
OC 21 '00			

DEMCO 38-296

The New Explorer's Guide to Maps and Compasses

Percy W. Blandford

TAB BOOKS
Blue Ridge Summit, PA

FIRST EDITION
FIRST PRINTING

© 1992 by **TAB Books**.
TAB Books is a division of McGraw-Hill, Inc.

Library of Congress Cataloging-in-Publication Data

Blandford, Percy W.
    The new explorer's guide to maps and compasses / by Percy W.
Blandford.
      p.   cm.
    Includes index.
    ISBN 0-8306-3915-2   ISBN 0-8306-3914-4 (pbk.)
    1. Maps. 2. Compass. I. Title.
GA151.B54   1992
912—dc20   91-39088
                                                            CIP

TAB Books offers software for sale. For information and a catalog, please contact
TAB Software Department, Blue Ridge Summit, PA 17294-0850.

Acquisitions Editor: Kimberly Tabor
Book Editor: Susan D. Wahlman
Director of Production: Katherine G. Brown
Book Design: Jaclyn J. Boone
Cover Photo by Susan Riley, Harrisonburg, VA   PFS

Contents

A Note to Adults

Some of the activities in this book require adult supervision. I have noted in the text where the child should ask for assistance. However, you must determine the amount of supervision an individual child or group of children needs, based on age and experience.

Introducing
Maps & Compasses

WHEN THE EXPLORERS SAILED FROM EUROPE ON THEIR VOYAGES OF discovery 500 years ago, they had fairly accurate compasses and were able to determine latitude with reasonable accuracy. However, they were unsure about longitude, so they would travel to the latitude of their intended destination and use their compasses to stay on that heading until they got where they wanted to go. You will come to appreciate their problems, as well as the solutions, as you read through this book.

As settlers became established in the New World, they built towns and roads and mapped them. As pioneers moved west, they mapped their progress until the whole country was mapped. If you want to go anywhere today, you expect a map to be available.

With a map and compass, you can re-create the thrilling experiences of the explorers and pioneers. If you are visiting a place for the first time, you might benefit from the mapping done by someone else, but you still will be finding your own way and experiencing the satisfaction of using your skills at map reading to know what lies ahead.

Most of us could find our way from point A to point B on a highway map, but mapping involves much more than that. Even a highway map can yield information that you did not know was there, if you study its symbols.

When you get away from roads, you learn to enjoy and rely on maps and compasses. You can find tremendous satisfaction in charting your way across wilder country by foot, horseback, or canoe.

Sea and air navigators rely on maps, charts, and compasses. You might not go into this kind of work, but knowing something of their methods can be interesting, and those methods might have other uses.

Maps and compasses need not be expensive. Very few other things are necessary. You even might want to make your own maps, as described in this book.

Discovering all the information on a map can be fun, and using it is not difficult. Using a compass is a skill soon mastered, and it lets you experience some of the thrills of exploration. Try some of the activities described in this book. You will not only enjoy yourself, you'll learn skills that always will be useful to you.

1

Knowing Your Maps

A MAP IS A PICTURE OF A PART OF THE SURFACE OF THE EARTH. IT might show your local streets, or your state, or a whole country, or the whole world. A map might remind you of a photograph taken from a high-flying airplane or even a satellite. In fact, such photographs are sometimes used as *aerial surveys* from which maps are made.

If the map is a picture of a very small amount of land, it might show widths of roads and shapes of houses. If it is a picture of a whole country, towns are represented by dots, and roads, if any, are just lines. In between are maps of moderate-sized areas. Plenty of detail is shown, but most things are represented by symbols, not actual shapes.

Any map is much smaller than the land it represents, even if it is a plan of your house and yard. The difference in size is called *scale*, which can be indicated in two ways. You can say 1 inch on the map represents a number of feet on the ground for example, 500. On a map of a state or country, one inch would have to represent many miles. In the example, you would say the map was to a scale of 1 inch to 500 feet. The other way of describing a map scale is to say how much smaller the map is than the land it represents. In the example, 1 inch represents 500 feet, or 6000 inches. This is shown on the map by a *representative fraction*. It is written $1/6000$ or 1:6000.

Map Types

If a map shows a large part of the earth's surface, it is called a *small-scale map*. You will find this type of map showing countries or continents in a school atlas. These maps cannot have much detail. A *large-scale map* shows a much smaller area, so it can contain a lot of detail. Large-scale maps might be road maps of states or maps for wilderness travelers. If a map has such a large scale that the widths of roads and outlines of houses can be shown, it is sometimes called a *plan*.

Every map does not show everything. If it did, it might be confusing to someone looking for only one sort of information. Most maps are made to suit particular needs. Standard maps on which the specialist maps are based are called "topographic survey maps. They are based on original government surveying. You can get topographic survey maps in various scales and sizes. These maps are the ones you need to explore wilderness country.

Maps are broadly divided into *political maps* and *physical maps*. A political map shows towns, roads, railroads, *boundaries*, and other man-made features, without much reference to such things as hills and rivers. A physical map concentrates on heights, waterways, and other natural features, only referring to towns and roads to provide locations. You are probably familiar with your state's highway map. It might not have any indication of ups and downs, although your state might have some steep hills. A topographic or physical map of the area would show hills, but would not have as much information about roads.

If you know something about the area you are in, or are familiar with a road, you should have no difficulty turning the map to match the land it represents. If you have any problems, your best aid for turning a map the right way is a compass. You will find much about compasses in this book. You should treat a compass as an essential part of mapping if you are to get the most out of it—and exploring with map and compass can be a lot of fun.

Margin Information

When you pick up a map you probably look at places you know and see how they relate to each other and places you don't know. When you have done that, look at the *margin*. The map is drawn within a border, called a *neatline*. Around it is a fairly wide margin, or open space, that contains a lot of information. Besides scales and compass direction, you might find an explanation of symbols (called a *legend*), other important information, and the date of the last revision of the map.

What is in the margin is important to your understanding of the map. The scale tells you the proportion of the map to the ground it represents, so you can estimate or measure distances and judge the sizes of lakes, parks, counties, or states. The legend allows you to identify the positions of objects on the ground from the symbols on the map. You can not only identify roads, you can learn something about them from the way they are drawn. You can also learn a lot of information from the way waterways are drawn.

Also in the margin you will find one or more arrows indicating north. Many maps are drawn with north at the top. That is convenient and the way people tend to visualize a map, but sometimes maps must be laid out with north in a different direction. The compass arrow in the margin will tell you which direction is north. Always check the north direction on the map before using it to locate places or discover directions. If you will be using a compass with the map, knowing how the map is oriented by looking at the arrow in the margin is important.

The map might have lines of *latitude* and *longitude* across it, but more often only the ends of the lines will be marked in the margin. They show the position of places on the map in relation to the whole world. No two places have the same combination of latitude and longitude. If you discover the latitude and longitude of your home, it is unique. Many maps have grids for locating places listed in the index of *gazetteer*. Usually these grids are just marks in a margin—you have to imagine or draw lines across the map to use them.

See what maps you can find. Later, you will have to buy or borrow maps for trips and expeditions, but you probably can find several maps and discover details you have not thought about before now.

Visitor Maps

Does your town display an information map for the benefit of visitors? An information map shows the positions of the town hall, churches, museums, and other places of interest. These places are shown prominently so that anyone can pick them out at a glance. The main streets are also shown clearly so that a stranger can find directions to the places they want to visit. What other information can you find on the map? Is the top of the map north? You might not find any indication if it is, but if north is in another direction, you should be able to find an arrow or symbol giving its direction. Somewhere on the map should be a scale. Get to know it. Then you can quickly estimate on the map the distance between places. Estimate the actual distance between two places you know, then check the map. Until you get used to estimating, you might be surprised at the differences. Assume the map is right.

You might find an information map displayed at the entrance to a state park. This map also gives the location of important places, but compare the way it shows them with the way the town map does. The maps use different symbols. The meanings of some will be obvious, but a key or legend on each map should explain meanings. The town map shows streets. The park map probably will show unsurfaced roads and trails as well. See how the differences between surfaced roads and trails are shown. The scales of the two maps also might be very different. See how this difference affects the amount of information that can be included. Each map has a different purpose. The town map shows how to find places of interest. The state park map is a guide to recreation. See how these different needs affect the way the map is made.

Other Maps

Look at the maps in your school *atlas*. Nearly all of them will have north at the top. Look through the pages. You might find a country that fits a page better another way. Check its north arrow. Compare scales. If all of the United States fits on one page, its scale must be much smaller than that used for England on the same size page. See if you find the country drawn to the smallest scale and that drawn to the largest scale. Notice how much more detail can be put on the large-scale map.

You can find maps in unexpected places. A local diner might use throwaway paper place mats with a map on them. Look at one. It most likely will be very inaccurate. It is intended as decoration, not for finding your way. Many advertisers and event organizers produce maps, usually to show you how to find their addresses. See how, on a good map, the essential information is there and you can follow through the route. A poor map might be confusing because of unnecessary detail, unclear directions at turns, and no indication of distance or scale. Think about how you would have drawn a map for the same purpose.

At one time you could get free road maps at gas stations. Now you will have to pay, but they are almost certainly the cheapest road maps you can get. Your state publishes a general map of the state, with road information and much more. You should be able to get one free, either at a highway welcome station near a state border or by mail.

Collect maps. If you have a variety from several sources, you can compare the ways their makers prepared them and see what details you can find on them. Two maps of the same area should have the same distances and place names, but note how one map gives certain details which the other ignores, depending on what the mapmaker thinks the reader wants. You might start adding information about places you know on a local map. Where does your scout troop meet? Do you have a favorite fishing or boating spot?

2

Symbols
& Scales

I F YOU WANT TO SHOW A FRIEND HOW TO GET TO A CAMPGROUND, your home, or some other place, you might sketch parallel lines for a road and a solid or broken line for a track, with dots for houses and places that mark turns or key points, probably with a note beside each explaining what they are. If you want to explain distances, you probably will tell your friend, "it is two miles from there to there," or write it on the sketch.

You have made a map. What the expert mapmaker does is only an extension of what you have done. A mapmaker is called a *cartographer*. Cartography is the science and art of making maps. You could say you are a cartographer when you draw your sketch map. Cartographers have ways of showing things on maps so that they can be recognized and interpreted. They use *symbols*. You can discover more than you might expect from some symbols, if you relate them to the examples shown in the legend, which is usually in the margin of a sheet map or at the front of an atlas.

Roads

If a map is very large-scale, the drawn outline of a road might match what it looks like on the ground, but on most maps, roads are shown with parallel lines. Many maps use color. Red is the usual color for roads, but you might find green or yellow inside black lines. You might check with the legend of each particular map, but some ways of indicating different types of road are shown in FIG. 2-1A. Even if the map does not show heights, it

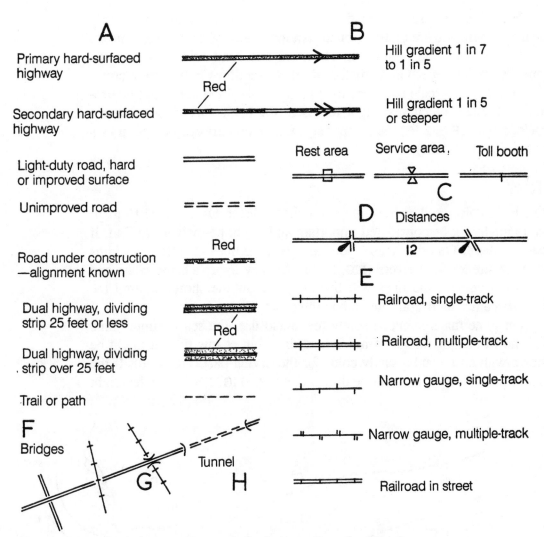

A

Primary hard-surfaced highway

Secondary hard-surfaced highway

Light-duty road, hard or improved surface

Unimproved road

Road under construction —alignment known

Dual highway, dividing strip 25 feet or less

Dual highway, dividing strip over 25 feet

Trail or path

Red

Red

Red

B

Hill gradient 1 in 7 to 1 in 5

Hill gradient 1 in 5 or steeper

C

Rest area   Service area   Toll booth

D Distances

12

E

Railroad, single-track

Railroad, multiple-track

Narrow gauge, single-track

Narrow gauge, multiple-track

Railroad in street

F
Bridges

G Tunnel **H**

Fig. 2-1. *Map symbols can tell you much about roads and railroads.*

might have symbols to show steep hills (FIG. 2-1B). The *gradient* 1 in 5 means that in a distance of 5 feet the road drops 1 foot in the direction of the arrow. Some places of interest to motorists might be marked along a road (FIG. 2-1C). Distances along a road might be given between marked points (FIG. 2-1D). In some states, exits on large roads are numbered according to their mileage from the state border, and these numbers are shown on the map. Try following a road on a map and see how much you can find out about it from symbols and the way it is drawn.

You might not use a railroad, but one can be very useful in positively locating where you are on the ground. An indication of the type of railroad (FIG. 2-1E) helps you identify it. How rail and road bridges are shown depends on the scale. On a small-scale map, the lines will merely cross. On a rather large-scale map, the road going under the other might be broken (FIG. 2-1F), or curves might represent the bridge which goes over a track or road (FIG. 2-1G). For a tunnel, the hidden part can be drawn as a dotted line (FIG. 2-1H).

Water

Blue is the color used on most maps to indicate water. On a motorist's map, rivers might not be considered important and might be difficult to find, if they are there. On other maps, you can find blue lines of different widths showing streams and rivers (FIG. 2-2A). As they approach the coast and become *estuaries*, the lines will broaden to show the shoreline until the water becomes an overall blue along the coast.

On some maps intended solely for inland use, the sea is simply blue with no further markings. If much land dries out at low tide, it might be shown with a line and a sandy color for the drying part (FIG. 2-2B). If the drying part is rocky, it might be drawn that way (FIG. 2-2C). Depths might

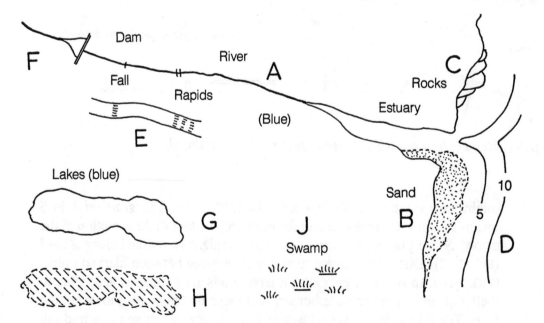

Fig. 2-2. *Details of water can be shown on a map in several ways.*

be shown with lines broken by figures indicating the *soundings* on a line (FIG. 2-2D). The legend will tell you what the figures represent.

On inland waters, what might be shown and how depends on the scale. Canoeists want to know about waterfalls or rapids (FIG. 2-2E). If the river is dammed, a line or road across marks the end of the pond or lake formed (FIG. 2-2F). A lake is shown blue inside its outline (FIG. 2-2G). If it sometimes dries out, the outline is broken and blue hatched lines fill the area (FIG. 2-2H). If the scale is large enough to show swamps, they might look like reed beds (FIG. 2-2J).

If your map is intended for people using water as well as dry land, it might have other symbols. Check the legend. Details at sea are only provided on a land map for the interest of those ashore. If you want to go boating, you need a nautical chart.

Landmarks

If you can see a church spire or water tower in the distance, its identification can help you locate your position on the map. Maps show isolated features that can be useful as landmarks. In a town, the position of a church could help you orient yourself.

Symbols might be representational, such as a church or windmill or pump (FIG. 2-3A). For others (FIG. 2-2B), you might have to check the legend. Telephone or raised pipelines (FIG. 2-3C) can be good visual identification points. If the scale is large enough, isolated buildings might be marked, but don't count on finding all buildings on a map.

From what you have discovered so far, you now can look at a map and find things you once did not know were there. How many churches can you find? Wind pumps and tanks might be rare in your area, but you might be able to find one. What about roads? The map can tell you if a back road has a hard surface and if it would make a good shortcut. When you get to a

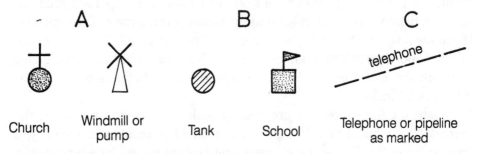

Church   Windmill or pump   Tank   School   Telephone or pipeline as marked

Fig. 2-3. *Symbols are used to show individual features.*

bridge, will the road go over or under the railroad? Does the railroad have one or more tracks? Amaze your friends with your knowledge of a place before you get to it.

Scales

If you have a piece of paper 12 inches across and you want to make a sketch map on it to show the route between two places 10 miles apart, you instinctively adjust the sizes you draw roads and other features to fit the paper. Although you might have not realized it, you have adopted a scale.

You mark the two key places about 10 inches apart, representing 10 miles on the ground. Your scale is 1 inch to 1 mile. If you want to make a representative fraction of it, you need to know the number of inches in 1 mile, which is 63,360. Since you are only sketching approximate sizes, you can simplify it to 60,000. You can say the scale of your map is 1:60,000, meaning the distance on the ground is 60,000 times as great as it is drawn on your map. Remember, those are the two ways of describing map scale. Many mapmakers favor the representative fraction, but knowing what 1 inch represents helps you estimate distances or measure them with an ordinary ruler.

You also should get to know metric measurements. Many parts of the world use the kilometer instead of the mile. A kilometer is 1000 meters. A meter can be divided into centimeters and millimeters. Everything is decimal (in units of 10), which makes proportions easy to follow. A kilometer equals about $5/8$ mile, so kilometers are about 5 miles. A meter is about 39 inches; about $2^1/2$ centimeters equal 1 inch. On most foreign maps, you find only a metric scale. Fortunately, many American maps show scales in kilometers as well as the usual miles, so you can compare them and learn the differences.

Measurements in both systems are shown in the appendix at the back of this book. For practical purposes on the ground, the important relationship to remember is that 5 miles is approximately the same as 8 kilometers. If you see a sign that says you will meet road repairs in 400 meters, you can call that 400 yards without noticing much difference. When measuring on a map, you can estimate that 12 inches equals 300 millimeters or 250 millimeters is 10 inches.

Maps are published to a great many scales. The larger the scale, the more detail can be shown, but the larger number of sheets you need if you want to travel far. For walking, you might be best served by a map with a scale of 1:62,500, which means 1 mile is represented by a little more than 1 inch. A person driving a car would cross the land shown on one of these sheets in a short time. The motorist needs a much smaller scale, possibly 1:500,000, or about 8 miles to 1 inch. That size still should have enough detail to show the features a motorist needs.

The margin of a map will have a note about the scale and a drawing of the scale, which you can use to transfer measurements. How this scale is marked depends on the proportion. On a walker's map, the scale would be marked in miles and fractions of miles. On a map of a country, the scale might represent tens or hundreds of miles. Besides a scale of miles, you might find a metric one or a scale in *nautical miles*. A nautical mile equals 6080 feet. This measurement is used by flyers as well as navigators at sea.

Make sure you understand the divisions of the scale you are using. Zero is usually not at the end of the scale. Whole divisions are marked to the right of zero and smaller parts or fractions are marked to the left (FIG. 2-4A). When measuring, take in all the whole divisions you can, then add fractions to make up the total (FIG. 2-4B). If more than one scale is drawn on the map, the zeros line up (FIG. 2-4C) so you can compare distances.

A simple way to measure a distance on a map is to mark the edge of a piece of paper (FIG. 2-4D) and put it against the scale (FIG. 2-4E). If it is a winding road, mark a section at a time, so the total length adds up as close as possible to the total distance along the road (FIG. 2-4F). If you have a pair of dividers or compasses, you can step along the road in a similar way (FIG. 2-4G), then step the same number of times along the scale line. You could bend a piece of string to shape along a road or river, then straighten it along the scale to learn the distance.

Map measures are also available. With one type, you run a little wheel on a threaded rod along the route, then run it back again along the scale to read the distance. With another type, the running wheel operates a pointer on a dial which reads the inches or scale distances.

Try measuring distances on a map. Compare the distance along a road or trail with the straight-line distance. You can check your results on a road with the odometer of a car. The mileage might be even greater since a map cannot show every minor twist in a winding road.

A scale drawn in the margin of a map is usually fairly short in relation to the distance across the map. Estimating distances of places shown a long way apart can be difficult. It will help if you know the scale distances of larger parts of the paper. Measure the scale lengths of the top or bottom border and a side border and write it in the margin. These numbers will give you lengths to compare with the distances you want.

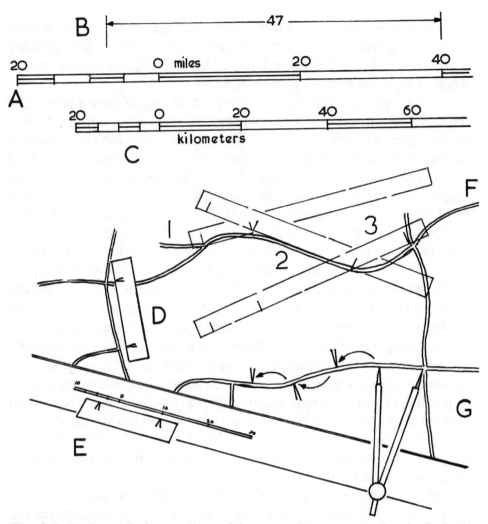

Fig. 2-4. *Scales might be in miles or kilometers. Distances can be checked with marked paper or dividers.*

Most maps are carried folded. Measure the scale lengths of the folds (FIG. 2-5A). If you remember these scale lengths, you can compare estimated distances between places without fully opening the map.

Because these references on the map are part of the map, you cannot place these longer scales against what you want to measure. If you are carrying more than one map, you can draw an extended scale on the back of one map for use on the other. It need only be the main marks. If the main scale shows every 4 miles, your longer one can do the same. If you need smaller divisions, you can refer to the detailed end of the main scale or esti-

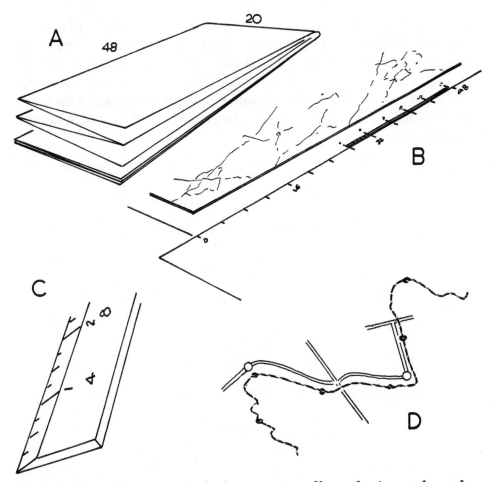

Fig. 2-5. *Edges of map, a marked ruler, or a piece of knotted string can be used to check map distances.*

mate them. Put the paper edge against the scale and mark matching divisions. Do this for as far as you think you will need (FIG. 2-5B). Number the marks.

You also can make a scale on the edge of a notebook that you always carry. If you have more than one scale, label them to avoid using the wrong one. If the scale happens to match divisions on a rule, as it would if it was 4 miles per inch, you could add mile marks to existing divisions to create a scale rule (FIG. 2-5C). On many maps, the divisions will not match inches exactly, although you might use inches for short distances with a fair degree of accuracy. In that case, you can mark the back of the rule in the same way as suggested along the edge of a piece of paper.

A useful measure is a piece of string at least as long as the diagonal of your map. Tie knots at scale distances. You cannot work to find limits. The spacing will depend on the scale. Perhaps every 10 scale miles will do, then you can bend the string along roads or trails to get a close idea of distances (FIG. 2-5D). This string measure takes up the least space for carrying. You might even use the cord that you hang around your neck to carry your compass.

3

How High Is It?

YOU CAN LOOK AT A MAP AND DISCOVER THE DISTANCE BETWEEN two points by using the scale. What the scale does not tell you is if hills and valleys lie between the points. Some parts of the country might have considerable ups and downs, so much that you cannot take a direct route and have to go around.

The only way a map could include hills and valleys to the same scale as distances would be to make a model. You might have seen such a model at the visitor center of a national park or similar place, but obviously you cannot carry one of these bulky models around with you. Heights have to be shown on your map in some other way.

On some maps, hills are shown by *relief shading*, usually with the shadows drawn as if the sun was shining low from the left side of the map. This method cannot be very precise, but you might find it on a map that is intended to be mainly pictorial or decorative and might have only a few isolated hills. The shading might be done in color or with close lines, called *hatching*. You could use this idea on a sketch map, but for serious mapping, you need a more accurate method.

Contour Lines

Heights are shown on a *topographic map* by *contour lines*. A contour line is drawn through points which are all at the same height or *elevation*. When you understand contour lines you can get a good idea of the terrain, or shape of the land—how steep hills are and how the hills and valleys will look when you get there.

Cut a big potato across lengthwise and stand half on its flat surface (FIG. 3-1A). Be careful not to cut towards yourself. If you need help, ask an adult. Imagine that the potato half is a model hill. Cut the potato into slices parallel with the base, all at about the same spacing, even if the top slice comes away quite thin (FIG. 3-1B). Place the bottom slice on a piece of paper and trace its shape. Do the same with each of the slices, placing it inside the first outline close to its correct relative position (FIG. 3-1C) Each line you have drawn represents the shape of the potato at the level of the slice a certain height above the base. You have drawn contour lines of the half potato.

Put the parts of the potato back together and compare it to the contour lines. If you only had the contour lines as a guide, you could see by the

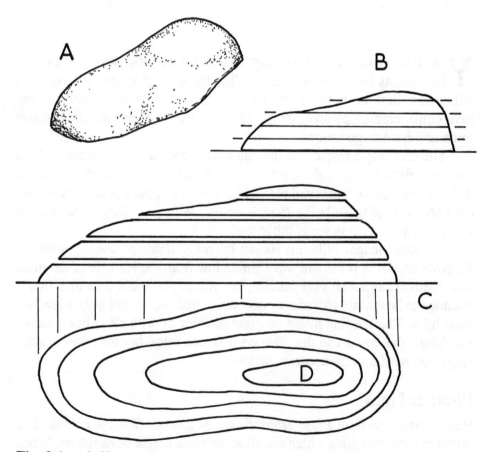

Fig. 3-1. *A half potato cut into slices shows how contour lines work.*

closeness of the lines that the slope close to the base is steep, but further up the spacing is greater, so the surface has a gentler slope. The highest part is not central, and its surface is a flattish curve (FIG. 3-1D).

You can think of contour lines as slices through the ground at certain heights, just like the potato. From their spacing and shape, you can picture rises and falls, peaks and valleys, plains and meadowlands, as well as the possibility of traveling in a particular direction.

Contour lines on a map are not always easy to find, particularly if the map has many other features, such as roads, towns, railroads, and all the other signs of a populated area. If your map is of wilderness area, contour lines will be more obvious. Even then they might be apparent only if the map is of hilly country. The lines might be rather faint compared with the lines of other features. On many maps the lines are brown.

Heights indicated by the contours are distances above sea level. Because of tides, the actual sea level varies, but mapmakers use an agreed level. This level does not matter to you because you are only concerned with the differences in height between one place and another. You can often tell whether slopes are up or down from the arrangement of contour lines, as in the potato drawing, but even then the lines might represent a hollow instead of a hill, if nothing else guided you.

Heights are shown by figures inset in the lines. These numbers might be feet, meters, or some other measurement. A note in the margin of the map will tell you. If the map represents fairly flat land with few contours, you might find a figure in every line, but in an area with moderate ups and downs, only every fourth or fifth contour line would have a figure. This *index contour* might be slightly thicker to make it easier to find (FIG. 3-2A). In the legend or margin of the map, you should find some information on the spacing of contour lines. The vertical spacing depends on the scale of the map—a map of a whole state cannot have contour lines at intervals as close as a map intended for wilderness travel across 20 miles.

If you were able to walk along the ground represented by a contour line, you would not go up or down. Although you may not be able to keep exactly to the route, this information might help you decide your best way around a hill. You might find signs of a trail made by animals doing the same thing.

Steepness

If you intend to go up or down a hill, the contour lines show you steepness. Lines that are wide apart mean a moderate slope (FIG. 3-2B). If they are

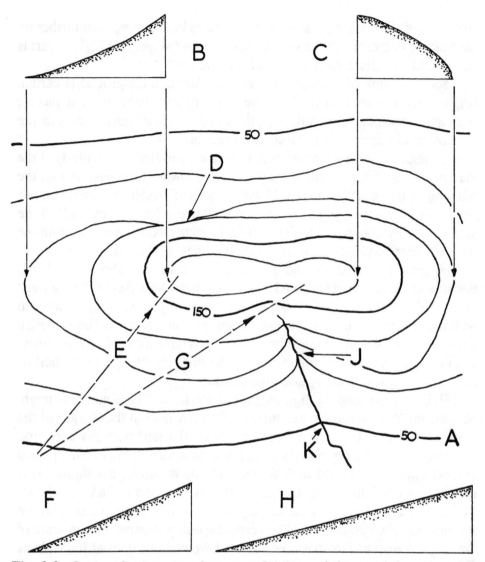

Fig. 3-2. *Contour line spacing shows you the types of slope and the amount of gradient.*

close, you might have to scramble up a steep slope (FIG. 3-2C). Lines that run together mean a near sheer drop or cliff (FIG. 3-2D).

Railroad tracks are laid so that slopes are always moderate. The curves in a track going across your map will show how the track was built to take advantage of land that does not vary much in elevation. Contour lines will confirm this observation and enable you to picture the form the land takes. If a track goes through a tunnel, the land over it must be high. If the track has a bridge, it must go over a hollow, probably a valley with a stream or river.

If you decide to go straight up a hill (FIG. 3-2E), you can see from contour lines how steep it is at a particular point (FIG. 3-2F). If you decide to go diagonally up the hill (FIG. 3-2G), the distance is longer, but the slope should be easier to walk (FIG. 3-2H). Remember that close contours mean steep slopes and wider spacing mean shallower slopes

Indications of water on a map help interpret heights and slopes. Water might be level, as in a lake, or it might flow from high to low ground, as in a stream or river. A stream will cross contour lines. If contour lines curve back upstream, the water has worn a groove (FIG. 3-2J). If the contour line across the stream changes only slightly, the ground is hard enough to resist wearing away (FIG. 3-2K). You might have to jump across a stream where it is deeply grooved, while you could wade across the other part.

Some maps use *layer tinting*—colors between contour lines. These maps are mostly physical maps that show the shape of the land, with less regard for man-made features. A graduated color code will be indicated in the margin. This code, with darker colors at the highest peaks, is a big help in visualizing the country.

If a lake or a large river estuary is on the map, contour lines might be continued underwater. These lines are called *soundings* and indicate parts of the bottom all at the same depth. The soundings, which are usually indicated by dark blue lines, might or might not be at the same intervals as land contours. Check in the map margin. One unit of depth, less likely to be used near land, is the *fathom* (6 feet).

If you have a map marked with contour lines, whether it is of an area you know or not, you can check the ups and downs. You can see if a road is steep, which can be important if you plan to cycle. You can check if you should be able to see something from the top of a hill or if another rise in between would block your view. If you want to walk between two places, would the direct way mean some climbing? Would it be easier to go around a longer way? If a stream is broad and shallow in one place, but deep and narrow somewhere else, which ought to be the better place to cross? Where are the highest points on the map? Can you see them from where you are, to use as guides to navigation?

Hills as Navigational Guides

Hills and valleys cannot usually provide as precise guides to map setting and route planning as church spires or tanks, which can be pinpointed exactly. If a hill goes to a peak, you might get a reasonably precise bearing, but usually hills are rounded and may extend at the same height for a long way, so they cannot give you more than a general direction. Even then, hollows, particularly the course of a river, might appear as a cleft in the hill. If a pass runs between two hills, it can usually be seen in the contours on the map and in your sight when you look that way.

If a mountain range is considerably higher than the surrounding country, you might be able to see it from a long distance away. However, check the height where you are. A peak at 6000 feet is high, but it doesn't look as high if you are already standing at 4000 feet. Except for these distant higher places, limit your interest in contours, and the heights and hollows they represent, to about 20 miles. Practice estimating distances up to that amount. Anything farther is liable to be indistinct, and you may be deceived when you try to visualize a distant place from map contour lines.

An isolated hill is fairly easy to identify, even if it does not rise very high (FIG. 3-3A). You can take a *bearing* on it with sufficient accuracy to set your map. If you see a range of hills that is mostly within one contour level, you can only get a general direction, but quite often the height will break through the next contour level for a short way. If that happens you can get a more accurate bearing (FIG. 3-3B). The height may go down as well as up. Look for a stream marked on the side of the hill. That could be a hollow (FIG. 3-3C) that you can see at a distance.

You should be able to picture a range of distant hills from the contour information. As you look around the horizon, you should see breaks between hills. These breaks might be river courses or just gaps left as the earth's crust settled a long time ago. If you check contour lines, the gaps should show up as spaces between higher lines (FIG. 3-3D). In a developed area, you probably will find roads and rail tracks going through the pass. You might see traffic moving, or other evidence that will help you, even if you cannot see the tracks.

Practice with a map marked with contours in a place where you can look in many directions, preferably all around you. Locate your position on the map and set the map and set the map fairly accurately in relation to the ground. If you see an obvious hill in one direction, compare it with the contour lines on the map. You can find both the height at your location and the height of the hill from the map. The difference between these figures it how much higher the hill summit is above you. If the contour lines show a hollow between you and the hill, you can work out how far you will go down and up if you walk directly to the hilltop.

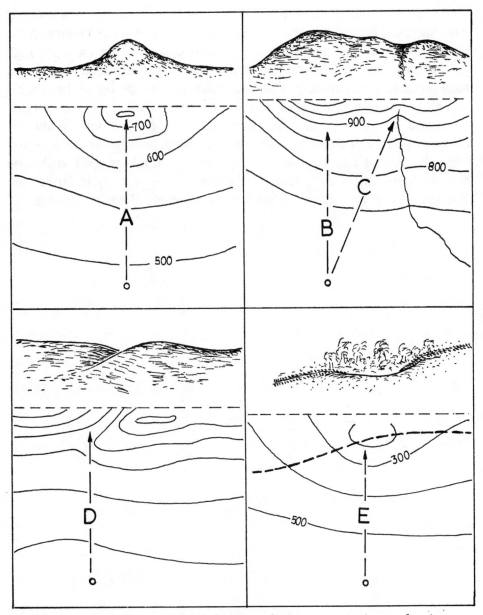

Fig. 3-3. *From the arrangement of contour lines, you can picture the view you expect.*

If a range of hills forms part of the horizon, the contour lines on the map will show them and you can discover the heights of each hill and how far each one is. You might be surprised at the distance. Hills might overlap each other in your view. Check how far they are apart. If the farther hill is higher, you should see its peak. If the contour lines show that it is lower, it will disappear behind the nearer hill. If it does not, you are looking in the wrong direction. If a tunnel for rail or road is marked on the map, high ground must cover it. Even if you cannot see the tunnel, the direction of a road might show where it is. Can you locate it from the lay of the land?

Hollows are not as easy as hills to see at a distance, but you can discover evidence of where they should be. Land you can see will dip towards the hollow. If water is in the hollow, foliage might be brighter there, or you might be able to identify water-loving trees. A track or road visible on higher ground might disappear for a while and be seen again farther on. You should find indications of this hollow in contour lines (FIG. 3-3E).

4

Which Way?

FOR MOST OF THE TIME THAT HUMANS HAVE BEEN ON EARTH, MANY people assumed it was flat. If you never go very far from home, your immediate area does seem to be flat. Even in the days of great explorers such as Columbus, most crew members were afraid they would fall off the edge of the earth. Not until the mid-1700s, when Captain James Cook sailed west until he got back where he started, did people accept that the world was round.

Those early explorers knew about north and south, even if they were unsure about where the actual poles were. Although you can get a lot of information out of a map alone, it is much more useful to you if you can relate its position and the ground it represents to north and south. Although finding north and south can be done without one, the instrument you really need is a compass. A map and a compass go together—and you can have a lot of fun using the two.

The Chinese are credited with discovering that a free-swinging magnet will settle on a north-south line. They used naturally magnetic iron ore, called *lodestone*, and floated it on a little boat in a bowl of water. They used this floating magnet as the first compass for navigating at sea. Modern magnetic compasses use the same principle, even is some of them look much more complicated.

You are unlikely to find a piece of lodestone, but you can make a compass very similar to the original Chinese one by using a steel sewing needle. Use one end of any magnet to stroke the needle many times one way along its length. Do not stroke back. You can check that the needle is mag-netized by using it to pick up a steel pin.

Carefully slice a thin piece off a bottle cork, or have an adult do it for you. Balance the needle on the cork slice and float it in a plastic or glass bowl of water. It will swing from side to side, but should eventually point north and south (FIG. 4-1A).

Another way of making a sewing-needle compass is to hang the needle by a hair. Use a fairly long hair and join it at the balance point of the needle with a blob of modeling clay or chewing gum (FIG. 4-1B). If you hold the other end of the hair, the needle with swing and then settle pointing north and south. You can take this simple compass with you and set a map by it if you are patient enough to wait for the gyrating to finish.

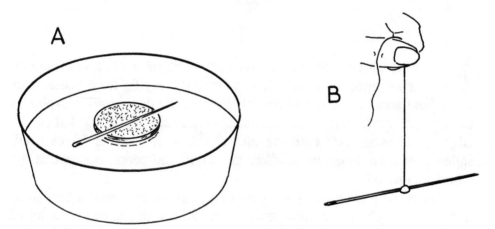

Fig. 4-1. *You can make a simple compass by floating or hanging a magnetized needle.*

Compasses

In a modern simple magnetic compass, the flat steel needle pivots on a point and is prevented from falling off by a transparent cover. The case is brass or plastic because these materials are nonmagnetic and will not affect the direction of the needle (FIG. 4-2A and B). Basic compasses of this type once were hidden in tunic buttons of wartime aviators, so if they had to bail out of their planes they could start navigating their way out of enemy territory.

You can buy a simple compass of this type, but a better one has a sealed case with the needle rotating in alcohol or another liquid. The liquid reduces the tendency of the needle to swing so that it quickly settles to point

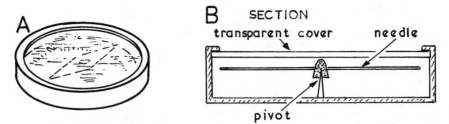

Fig. 4-2. *A simple compass has a magnetized needle pivoting at its center.*

north. This kind of compass is particularly valuable if you want to read the compass while moving, like when you are walking or paddling a canoe.

Fortunately, only iron and steel attract a compass needle and deflect it from pointing north. Other metals and materials do not affect it. Keep iron and steel well away from a compass when you read it. It can be deflected by the steel casing of a car. Do not overlook a steel belt buckle or a knife on your belt.

Compass Directions

Besides north, the other *cardinal points* are east, south and west (FIG. 4-3A). Midway between each pair of these points are four others made by putting the adjoining cardinal points together—northeast, southwest, etc. (FIG. 4-3B). Make sure you know these eight points. You don't need to go further with points. The oldtime square-rigger sailor used a complex system of other points. Today, you can use degrees, taken clockwise around the dial.

If you have a hard time remembering east and west, imagine facing the sun (south). East has an initial letter alphabetically before west. Left has an initial letter before right. The early initials go together (L and E) and so do the later ones (R and W).

Degree markings start at north, which is 0° and 360°. On a large compass, each degree calibrations could be shown, but in hand compasses they are marked every two degrees (FIG. 4-3C), which is as close as you will need to work in normal map and compass uses.

Compass makers arrange compass markings in three different ways. The marks could be in the base of the case with the needle swinging over them (FIG. 4-3D). They might be on the rim, or *bezel*, of the case, so the needle points at them (FIG. 4-3E). One of the more popular compact compasses for use with road and wilderness maps, as well as for the sport of orienteering (see chapter 10), is made in several forms by Silva. This type

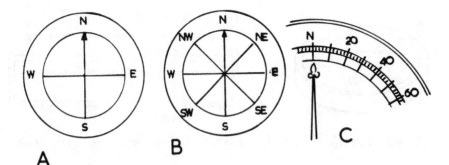

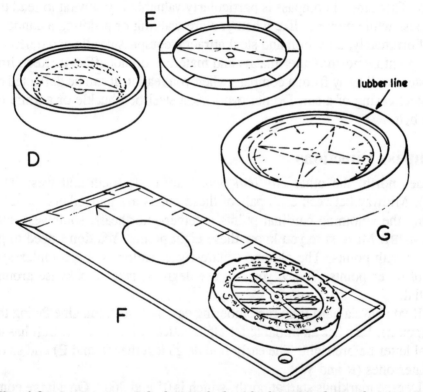

Fig. 4-3. *A compass might be marked with the main lettered points or with degrees. Bearings might be marked on the inside bottom of the compass, on the rim, or on a card attached to the needle.*

of compass has a liquid-damped needle in a rotating case on an oblong base used for sighting bearings. The rim of the case has degree calibrations marked on it (FIG. 4-3F).

In the third type of compass, the markings are on a round *card*. The needle forms part of the card so they rotate together (FIG. 4-3G). Directional readings are made against a mark on the rim, called a *lubber line*. This type of compass is used for steering ships or aircraft. It is fixed so that the lubber line points in the forward direction.

For most of your map and compass work, you will find that the standard Silva compass, or a similar one, is all you need. For more advanced plotting of directions or precise navigating, you might want a *bearing* or *sighting compass*. They come in several forms, but each has a means of looking across the dial to get a sight on an object. Then you glance down through a prism or mirror to read the bearing.

Sun and Stars

If you are without a compass, you can still get an idea of compass directions from natural indicators. Moss grows more on the north sides of trees, foliage is stronger on the south side of a hill, and trees grow leaning away from the prevailing wind. These and other similar indications are only rough guides. If you can see the sun or stars, you can work much more accurately.

Because of the rotation of the earth, the sun appears to rise in the east and set in the west, following a southward arc through the sky. It is at its highest point at noon. Even without a watch, you can face the sun when it is at its highest point and know you are looking south. If you know the time, you can check that the sun appears in the south at noon, east at 6 A.M. and west at 6 P.M. At midnight it is north, but you cannot see it. If your state uses Daylight Savings Time, sun noon is at 1 P.M.

For an accurate north mark on the ground, set up a stick on a flat surface. Put a pebble at the end of the shadow it casts at noon (FIG. 4-4A). The pebble is directly north of the stick. If you cannot check the time, mark the ends of shadows with pebbles at intervals (FIG. 4-4B) around the time you judge the sun will be highest. The pebble marking the longest shadow will be the north one. The farther north you are, the longer the shadows will be and the easier it is to compare them. If you are on the equator, the sun will be directly over the stick at noon.

You can use a watch as a compass in two ways. Try them both. The watch must have hands and be correctly set. Ignore the minute hand. Point the hour hand at the sun. Divide the angle between that hour and noon (1 P.M. for Daylight Savings Time). This line through the center of the watch runs north and south (FIG. 4-4C). North is the direction away from the sun.

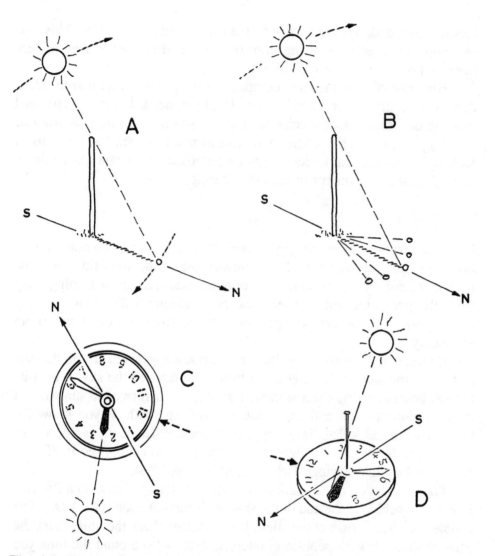

Fig. 4-4. *You can use a watch and the sun to find north.*

A problem with that method, particularly if you are using a small watch, is knowing when the hour hand points directly at the sun. A better way is to use something that casts a thin shadow, such as a knife blade on edge or a pin. Put this object over the center of the watch so that its shadow falls along the hour hand. Bisect the angle between the hour hand and noon (FIG. 4-4D). That line runs north and south, but you are working the other way—north is still away from the sun. Practice these methods and check your results with a compass, if possible. The watch method could be useful to you in the wild.

On a clear night, you can use the stars to find compass directions. Because of the rotation of the earth, the pattern of the stars appears to move, but fortunately the North Star, or Pole Star, seems to hang over the North Pole and all other stars seem to rotate around it. The North Star can be found if you are north of the equator. Those who live south of the equator (and cannot see the North Star) are not so lucky because they do not have a central pole star and have to use a less definite method to find south.

If you can locate the North Star and face it, you then must be facing north. Some stars appear brighter than the North Star, but it is fairly easily identified by using other stars as guides. One constellation of seven stars is usually easy to pick out (FIG. 4-5A). It has been given many names, including Great Bear, Plow, and Big Dipper. The two end stars can be used as pointers (FIG. 4-5B). If you extend a line through them six or seven times as long as their distance apart, you will find the North Star. As a check on your findings, look for five stars in a W formation (FIG. 4-5C). The center of the W points toward the North Star.

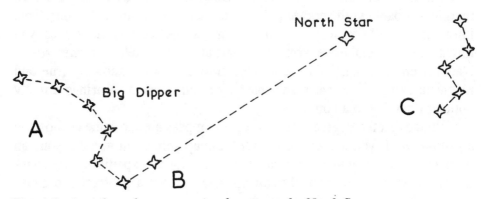

Fig. 4-5. *At night, other stars point the way to the North Star.*

Remember, the star pattern of the sky moves around the North Star, but the constellations always keep the same position relative to each other, even if at times the Big Dipper appears upside down or sideways. Directions to north are still the same.

Go outside on a clear night and find those vital constellations and the North Star. Stars are easier to see if you get away from street and house lights, especially the bright lights from a town center—the darker the sky, the clearer the stars. A moonless night is best for your first observation. Even if patches of cloud are about and you cannot see the North Star, estimating distance in the sky from the Big Dipper will give its location.

When you are in back country, getting directions from the sun and stars might be vital. You cannot have too many checks on direction, even if you have a compass. Without one, the sun and stars are important guides.

North and Magnetic North

A compass needle does not point directly to the North Pole. Instead, it points to the *magnetic pole*, which is in the far north of Canada. Because it is in the same general direction for anyone using a map and compass in America, the difference probably is not enough to bother about if all you want is a broad indication. Elsewhere in the world, this *deviation* or *declination* can be a lot greater and must always be considered. In some eastern states the declination is about 7° (FIG. 4-6A). If you want to work to accurate bearings, you must allow for this deviation when using your map. The magnetic pole moves slightly, but not enough to make a difference for most practical purposes.

The north direction might be shown by a simple arrow in your map margin, probably with another pointing to magnetic north (FIG. 4-6B). That information is all you need, but on some maps, particularly older ones, you might see very elaborate arrows or partial or complete *compass roses*. Nautical charts usually have complete compass roses, showing true and magnetic bearings so that a ship navigator can measure bearings directly without referring to a compass.

Notice that the degree markings on a compass are the same as those on a *protractor*. If you are at home with the map spread on a table, you can work out bearings with a protractor to prepare for an expedition (see chapter 5). Outdoors you probably can manage without a protractor because your compass will serve in a similar way.

When you first look at a map, take note of the north arrow. Although most maps have north at the top, don't assume that it is always so. Look for the north arrow, usually in the margin. Sometimes a map of a particular area fits on the paper better another way, especially if the area to be mapped is long and narrow in a direction that is not north and south. The compass arrow is then drawn to show north (FIG. 4-6C).

For example, a series of strip maps for a river might sprawl all over a map if it was to have only one compass direction. A canoeist is only interested in the river and not the country a long way from it, so parts of the river can be drawn in strips each with its own compass direction and indications where one strip overlaps the next (FIG. 4-6D). Drawing the map in strips brings the big sweeps of the river down to three manageable sections.

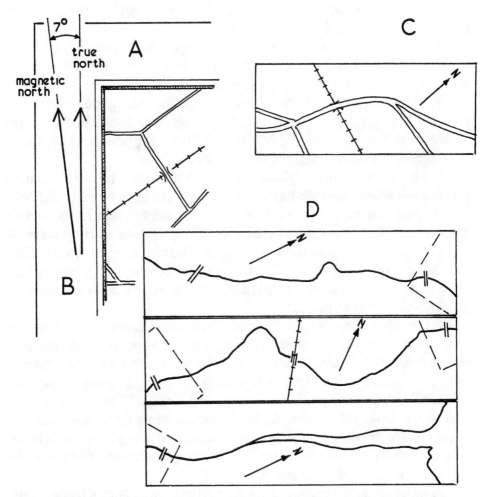

Fig. 4-6. *True north and magnetic north might be shown in the margin of a map, or a north arrow might appear on the map.*

Fun with a Compass

A compass is an interesting tool to use. You should become familiar with it and be able to use it without having to think too much about your actions. When you go into the wilderness, participate in an orienteering competition, or just want to check a road map, you need to be certain of what you are doing. You don't want to confuse east with west or read the south end of the needle instead of the north and go the wrong way. Use your compass frequently. Get used to its feel and action. Check bearings of familiar streets. Notice the bearings of a gate from your bedroom window. Look cross country at a church spire and read its bearing. All this practice adds up to experience, which is what you want.

Many practical exercises for using a compass are described later in the book, but now I'll tell you a few things to do that you will enjoy while becoming familiar with having a compass in your hands.

Walk around a block in town and take bearings along the streets. You probably thought the streets crossed squarely. Do they? If they were square, each bearing would be 90° or 270° from the previous one. Quite often they will be a few degrees off (FIG. 4-7A).

See if you can walk straight on a course. Start from a tree or something you can see when you look back. Decide on a compass bearing and hold the compass in front of you. Walk one hundred paces as near as you can on that bearing. Turn around and read the bearing of your starting point. It should be 180° from your outward bearing. Walking straight is very difficult. Most people veer to one side, so the return bearing will probably be a few degrees off (FIG. 4-7B). Try this exercise with your friends and see who can keep closest to a course.

You might arrange a treasure hunt. How complicated it is depends on your age and experience. Have it among trees or vegetation that is easily passed through, but that blocks the view of the destination. Use bearings and paces. Make your first treasure hunt fairly short. You might count off 40 paces on one bearing, 10 on another, and finally, 30 paces on another (FIG. 4-7C). Make the treasure fairly obvious to allow for different lengths of paces. The treasure might be a box containing enough candy bars for each competitor to have one. For older or more experienced friends, make the course longer and add more bearings.

A variation on the treasure hunt is to arrange two courses that are mirror images of each other (FIG. 4-7D). Put a marker at the destination where the two courses should meet. Send off two competitors and see which one can get closer to the mark.

You might want to lay out a compass pattern on the ground. You can place rocks on a piece of waste ground or build it into a garden. You might use flat stones set into the lawn so they do not interfere with the mower. Decide on a size, perhaps 6 feet across. Attach a string to a central peg with a stick tied at a radius of 3 feet. Scratch a circle on the ground with the stick (FIG. 4-7E). Stand with your compass over a stone at the center of the circle, sight the north position on the circle, and put a large stone or a group of stones there. Do the same with slightly smaller stones at south, east, and west (FIG. 4-7F). Check your accuracy so far by measuring. Distances

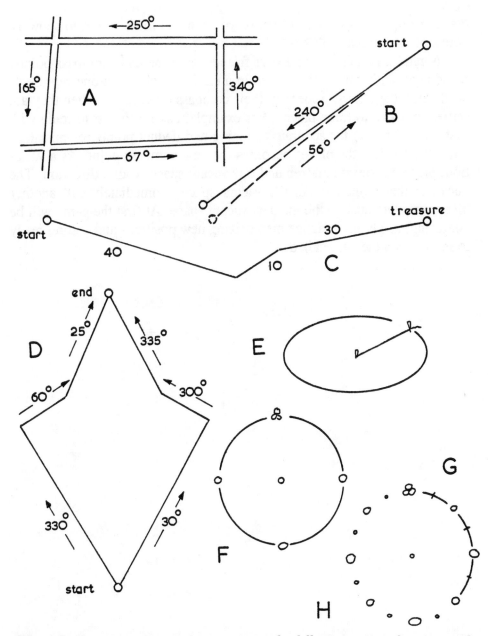

Fig. 4-7. *You can practice using a compass by following various bearings or by marking out a compass on the ground.*

between the stones should all be the same. Now sight for smaller stones on the circle at northwest, northeast, southeast, and southwest. Check that these points are halfway between the other stones on the circle (FIG. 4-7G).

You can stop at 8 compass points, or you can add more stones to show 16 points of the compass (FIG. 4-7H).

A game can help you and your friends learn the main compass points. Stand eight children evenly spaced in a circle. Decide that one represents north. Ask the others to identify their compass directions. When they are settled, ask two to trade places. For example, ask northwest to trade with east. Award points for accurate changing and deduct points for mistakes. After the change, the player becomes the new compass point. As a variation, play with seven children and one vacant space. Call a direction. The player at that point goes to the vacant space. Immediately call another direction, who must go the the new vacant space. At first the game will be confusing, as players practice memorizing new positions and getting ready to move when they are called.

5

Map & Country

IF YOU JUST WANT TO LOOK AT A MAP, YOU HOLD IT OR PUT IT ON A table in the most convenient position. It does not matter if its north point matches north on the ground or not. If you are in the open, whether in the wilderness or in town, and you want to use the map to find your way, you will find that working out directions is easier if the map is arranged the same way as the land it represents. Getting map and ground to match is called *orienting* or *setting the map*.

You will not always need to set your map, particularly if you have no doubt about where you are and the direction you have to go. If you are at a junction on an interstate and you know the town you are aiming for is 150 miles along the highway, you probably will not misread the map, whether you sit with it in a convenient position on your knees or get out of the car and turn the map the same way as the road.

At the other extreme, you must know how to set a map if you are in unmarked wilderness country and you do not know which way to go. In plenty of situations between these two examples, setting the map, possibly only approximately, will stop you from going the wrong way. If unmarked back roads or tracks cross or diverge, finding that point on the map and turning it the same way shows you the direction without any doubt. Even busy roads and street near a city center are more easily understood with the map set so that its layout matches the actual layout of crossings and junctions on the ground.

Setting a Map

Setting a map can be done in many ways. A compass is always useful, but if you can identify landmarks, you can use them. Unless you are in a desert you will, almost certainly, see something that you can also find marked on the map. It might be a road, track, isolated house, or hill. Skill in setting a map comes with the ability to use a combination of sights and compass, so that one or more extra methods can be used to confirm the results of the first method. In all mapping, you need to be able to check one action against another so that the results are confirmed.

If you know where you are on the ground and can find the same point on your map, you easily can set the map correctly. Suppose you are at a crossroads and a sign tells you the direction and distance of a town along one road. You can turn the map until the road to the town marked on it runs the same way as the actual road (FIG. 5-1A). Your map is set. Having set the map, you can look around for other things shown on the map and see if they are visible on the ground. Mapmakers show things that are prominent so they can be used as landmarks. Checking these other sights is always worthwhile, although in this case you probably have no doubts because of the road and town directions.

If you are away from roads, but know where you are, you might still be able to set the map using landmarks. Suppose you are at a viewpoint marked on the map. The map shows a water tank about 4 miles away. Can you see it? Estimate its distance to make sure you are not mistaken. Turn the map so that a line between the viewpoint and the tank on the map are in line with your sighting (FIG. 5-1B). Putting a pencil or other straightedge through the points on the map and sighting along it can be helpful (FIG. 5-1C).

If you are uncertain of your location, you run the risk of going in the opposite direction. Suppose you have been walking across country and come to a road or track that is marked on the map. Should you turn right or left? If the sun is shining, it cannot be north of you, so turn the map around so that its south marking is in the general direction of the sun, even if you do not have a watch to check the time. At night, if the North Star is visible, you can orient by it. Think back about the way you have come. That should tell you on which side you have approached the road or track. All this information need only be general—all you want to know is whether turn left or right on the road.

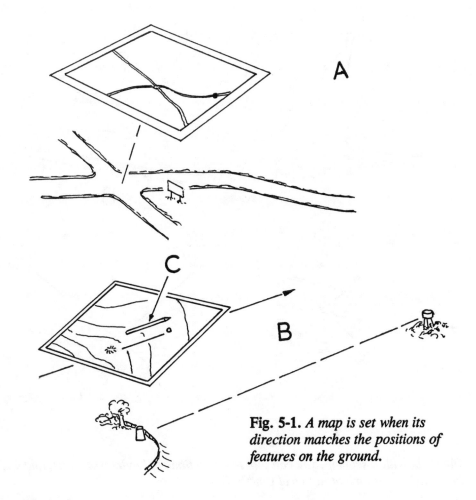

Fig. 5-1. *A map is set when its direction matches the positions of features on the ground.*

Landmarks

If you know where you are and can see a positive landmark, as in the first example, you can set the map to match the land so that you can plan your route. Suppose you only have a general idea of where you are on a fairly straight track. Turn the map so that the road shown on it runs the same way as the actual road. One bearing of a landmark, particularly if it is nearly square to your position on the road (FIG. 5-2A) should allow you to set the map by sighting with the aid of a pencil. Then you should have a good idea of where you are on the map and ground. A sighting of a second landmark will confirm the first finding (FIG. 5-2B). Move the set map about without turning it so that your sightings of the landmarks are as accurate as you can

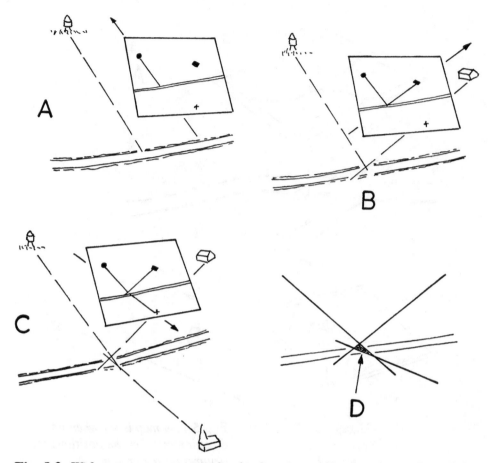

Fig. 5-2. *With a set map, you can plot the directions of landmarks (A, B, and C), but bearing lines might not meet exactly (D).*

get them. Do not expect your sight lines on the map always to cross exactly at the right spot on the map—you are aiming for a close approximation, which should be all you require.

If you can identify three landmarks, sight the third to confirm the results of the other two. The sight lines on the map are unlikely to coincide, but you will be within the little triangle made by their crossing (FIG. 5-2C). The triangle is what a nautical navigator calls a *cocked hat* (FIG. 5-2D).

You can practice map setting using features of the land that are marked on the map, even if they are town streets or land around your home, that you know well. You then will feel more confident when you get into country that you do not know. If you have a compass to use with the map, you should be able to work more accurately.

You can also set a map with a compass. If you have one with a rotatable bezel, make sure the needle is pointing at the north mark. Set the north mark to the sight line on the Silva compass base if you have one. Put the compass against the magnetic north arrow on the map and turn the map until the compass north and the magnetic north agree (FIG. 5-3A).

Another way to set a map with a compass is to put the compass over or alongside the border of the map, if it is arranged to north-south. Set the map by turning it until the compass shows the correct declination (FIG. 5-3B). If the compass does not have a transparent base, check that the degree readings at opposite sides of north and south are the same to verify that the compass is central on the border line. In many cases, setting the compass to true north and ignoring a small declination might be accurate enough for your purpose. If all you want to do is identify roads, differences of a few degrees do not matter. If you are navigating across unmarked wilderness, those few degrees might be important.

Since not all maps have north at the top, always check the compass arrow found in the margin or on a vacant part of the map itself. To set the map, you can place your compass on the arrow (FIG. 5-3A). You cannot use the compass on the map border if the border does not run north and south, unless you first discover the angle to magnetic north.

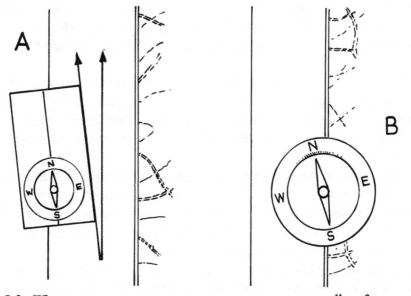

Fig. 5-3. *When you use a compass to set a map, you must allow for magnetic north.*

Using a Protractor

Sometimes you will want to transfer bearings to or from a map without orienting or setting it in relation to the land, as when the map is in the cabin of a boat or inside a house where you do not have a direct view of the surrounding land. You might want to discover bearings from the map before you go to the place where the landmarks are. In that case, you need to be able to measure magnetic degrees on the map. The best tool for measuring degrees is a protractor, like the one you might use for school geometry. Your protractor might be marked with degrees both ways around, but remember that for compass work you only use the markings going clockwise.

The compass itself could be used as a protractor, ignoring the needle and only using the degree markings on the rim, but a larger protractor might be easier to read a map. Use a soft pencil to *plot* bearings on a map, so that you can erase the lines easily.

Suppose you need to find the bearing of a hill from a bridge over a railroad so that when you go out to that bridge you will have no difficulty in identifying the hill from the others around you. Draw a light line between the bridge and the hilltop on the map. Draw a north-south line through the bridge symbol (FIG. 5-4A). Put a protractor on the north-south line with its center at the bridge symbol. Read the angle of the hilltop bearing (FIG. 5-4B). If you are working on a true north line, you must allow for declination. For this example, assume the declination to be 6°. The bearing reads 42°. You must add 6°, making 48° the compass bearing (FIG. 5-4C). If the map bearing had been west of north, you would need to subtract the declination.

When you get to the actual bridge, sight over your compass at 48° and you will see the hill. If you are using a Silva compass, set 48° on the rim over the sight line, turn the whole compass until the needle points north, then look over the central line or along one edge of the compass base (FIG. 5-4D) at the hill.

You can take a large number of bearings in this way so that when you go out into the actual area, you have the compass directions ready to use. Several hill or mountain peaks might be within view of your starting point. If you have already worked out the bearings, you can greet them as old friends, even if you have never been there before.

Try taking some local bearings. Don't assume that because a town 20 miles away from you is to the southwest, the road between is always southwest. Because of winding, parts might be 90° or more away from that. Survey sections of the road with your compass and check it against the map.

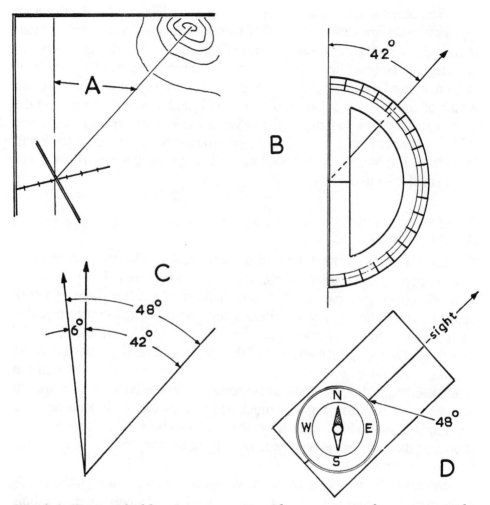

Fig. 5-4. *You can find bearings on a map with a protractor, then convert to the direction on the ground with a compass.*

Imagined directions might be very different from what they actually are. Since the Pacific Ocean is to the west and the Atlantic Ocean is to the east, you might assume that the Panama Canal runs west to east. Does it? Get out your atlas and check.

Now is also the time to get to know your map's symbols and contours. Perhaps you arrive at a road which you thought would have a hard surface and a downwards slope, when actually it is a dirt road with a steep upward gradient. It goes under a railroad, but you thought it went over. The stream you expected to wade is a broad lake, held back by a dam. The map would have told you all these things in advance.

First check a map against country you know. Notice how the different types of roads are shown. See what symbols are used for familiar landmarks. See how the steepness of a hill is indicated by the distance between crossings of contour lines. If you can remember these marks from your local roads and other features, you will know what to expect when you use a map of country you do not know. You will gradually learn to picture the land represented by getting all the information you can from a map. You will find yourself saying, "When we get around the next bend, a track will be to the left opposite a rest area," or "When we top the next rise we will see a small lake to our right."

Different Scales

You want to be able to read maps of different scales. The best way to learn about scale is to compare maps that include the same area. The large-scale map will cover only part of the small-scale one, yet the piece of paper might be about the same size. Look at the two maps and compare scales and symbols. The road between two towns might be just a line on a small-scale map. On the other map, part of the road might be shown as a divided highway and you might see some minor roads that are not shown on the small-scale map. Look at the contour details. On the large-scale map, the differences in elevation might be much less than on the small-scale map, so you might discover hills and valleys that did not rise and fall enough to be shown on the small-scale map because they came between the wider elevations of contours.

Symbols also might be different. Where a town was a dot on the small-scale map, its actual outline might be shown on the larger map. Symbols for some landmarks on the large-scale map are not shown at all on the other map.

If one of the maps has an inset of the street plan of a town, you will find a different mapping scene to understand. Look at the scale. Instead of 1 inch representing several miles, several inches might equal 1 mile. This larger scale means the inset can show much more detail with possibly, a whole new range of symbols. Roads might be drawn to scale widths, squares and other open spaces might be scale size, and buildings might be drawn to match their actual shape.

With maps at three different scales, you can compare what can be shown on each. After a while, you will be able to switch from one scale to another and picture what the details on the maps represent and have a better sense of proportion. For instance, you can compare the length of a highway on a map with one on another scale map or be able to imagine the height of a hill in relation to its contour lines.

6

Where Are You?

IF YOU ARE USING A MAP OF A FAIRLY SMALL FAMILIAR AREA, YOU should have no difficulty locating towns and features already known to you. Locating a place becomes more difficult if the map covers a large area, and you know the place you want to find is on it, but you don't know where. Even more difficult is getting the position of a town somewhere in a foreign country, when you might not even know how to find the country.

You can often get close to a spot if you know its general location in relation to someplace else. For instance, you might know that Blue Ridge Summit, Pennsylvania, is some way west of Philadelphia, or that the town you want is in Maryland and not a place of the same name in California. You still have to search, even if the area to explore has been limited. An index in an atlas might tell you the right map and get you close to the place you want, but in most cases you will have to search over an area of that map.

For locating a place exactly, you need to use imaginary lines crossing the map north to south and west to east. The closer these lines are, the easier locating places will be. You can describe a position as being at or near the crossing of two lines and go directly to it. On a worldwide scale, these lines are called *lines of longitude* (north to south) and *lines of latitude* (west to east). Large-scale maps of small areas might use other grids of lines with an index to locate every town in a state or even every street on a town plan.

Latitude and Longitude

The face of the earth has more water than land, so ocean navigators need to be able to find and use lines of latitude and longitude to know where they are. Finding these lines was quite a problem with primitive equipment in the early days of exploration, but it is a more exact science now and is used by planes as well as ships.

The earth is an almost true sphere or ball. The imaginary lines on the surface are found by measuring angles from the center of the earth. If you draw a line up and down through the center of the earth, its ends will be the North and South Poles. If you draw a line at 90° to that, it will hit the surface at the circumference halfway between the poles, which is the equator (FIG. 6-1A). The equator is regarded as 0° latitude and other lines of latitude are numbered north and south from that (FIG. 6-1B). The poles are at 90°.

Whole degrees are much too coarse for fine navigation. One degree is divided into 60 minutes. Each minute is further divided into 60 seconds. An angle can be abbreviated with degree (°), minute (′) and second (″) signs; for example, 35 degrees, 21 minutes, and 32 seconds north is written 35°21′32″N.

Beside the lines of latitude at degree intervals are specially identified lines. At the furthest points north and south of the equator that the suns rays fall vertically on the earth are the *Tropic of Cancer* (23 1/2 °N) and *Tropic of Capricorn* (23 1/2 °S). Around the North and South Poles the limits where the sun appears above the horizon every day of the year are marked by the *Arctic Circle* (66 1/2 °N) and the *Antarctic Circle* (66 1/2 °S) (FIG. 6-1C).

Lines of latitude, also called *parallels of latitude*, tell you how far north and south you are from the equator. To get an exact location, you need to be able to refer to similar lines crossing the equator at right angles. These lines are *meridians of longitude*. One of these meridians—the *prime meridian*—has been chosen as 0° and others are measured east or west from it. The prime meridian almost universally recognized throughout the world passes through Greenwich, near London, England. Positions on lines of longitude are described as west or east of Greenwich (pronounced "Grennich"). For instance, Washington, D.C., is 77°W of Greenwich (FIG. 6-1D). The *International Date Line* is on the opposite side of the earth from the prime meridian, at 180°.

No two places in the world have the same latitude and longitude reference. You can pinpoint a remote spot in China or give the position of your hometown, working to degrees, minutes, and seconds, if necessary.

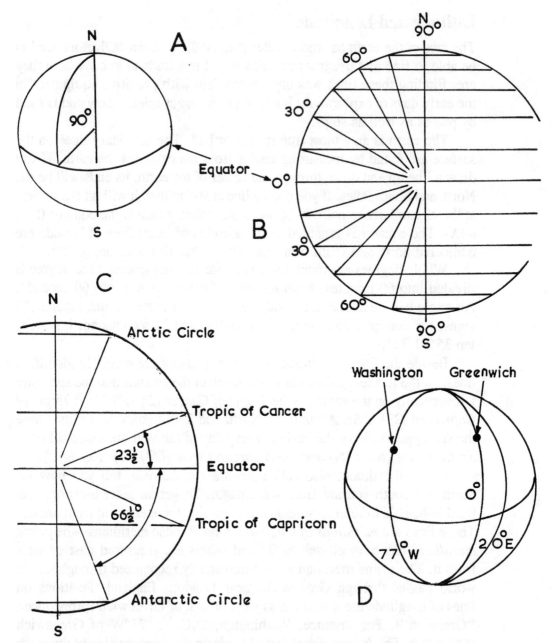

Fig. 6-1. *The equator goes around the center of the earth (A) and lines of latitude are parallel to it (B and C). Lines of longitude pass through the poles (D).*

The flat maps we use represent part of the earth's curved surface. The amount of flattening to cover an area 100 miles each way is not enough to matter. For a much bigger area, the curved surface of the sphere cannot be represented on a flat sheet without distortion. I'll deal with this problem in greater detail in chapter 8, but at this stage understanding latitude and longitude is easier if you look at a globe instead of a flat map.

Even a small globe will help, but if you can find a large one in your local library or elsewhere, you will see these lines drawn, and they look rather different from the way they are arranged on a flat map. See how the lines of longitude all go through the poles and lines of latitude are parallel with the equator.

The shortest distance between two places will not always be the route you would expect from drawing a straight line on a flat map. From London across the Atlantic to New York, the shortest route goes near Newfoundland. If you stretch a string from London to San Francisco, the shortest distance goes over the top of the world. Without a globe you would not expect this result.

Looking at places on a globe will help you understand how the flat map of your local area fits into the whole scheme. You will see how the lines of latitude and longitude marked on it are important references, but that you might not bother about them if all you want to do is drive along the interstate for 100 miles. However, if you want to go farther afield, you might be glad to know about them.

If you dealing with a world map, or even one of a group of countries, you probably have to refer to latitude and longitude. If you are using a map of your state or an even smaller area, you are not usually concerned with where the place is in relation to the rest of the world or even your continent. However, latitude and longitude will be there, possibly just as readings at a corner of the map or marks in the border to show where lines would cross the map. If a map is intended for navigation from the air, lines of latitude and longitude are marked more prominently.

National topographic maps are made in sections bounded by lines of latitude and longitude. Because lines of longitude get closer together as you travel north of the equator, such a map of a southern part of the United States covers a slightly larger area than one of the north. These maps are named for a prominent place somewhere on it.

Grids

Some maps, particularly those intended for motoring, use a system of *grid* markings for place identification that is not related to latitude and longitude. Not all systems are the same, so check the description in the margin or at the front of an atlas. Somewhere on the map or in the atlas should be an index of places. This index will list locations and give the page number of the appropriate map followed by an identification of a grid square. You are left to find the place in a comparatively small square.

In one grid system, squares of a convenient size are drawn over the map surface. They are given identifying letters one way and numbers the other way in the margin (FIG. 6-2). The atlas index will tell you which map has the town you want, followed by letter and a number. That limits your search to one square. For instance, Aytown and Beetown might both be identified as being in square B2. You will have to look among all the places in that square, but finding the towns should not be difficult.

Another system of *grid references* is more precise and might be used for military purposes or for locating places in remote areas, as well as for

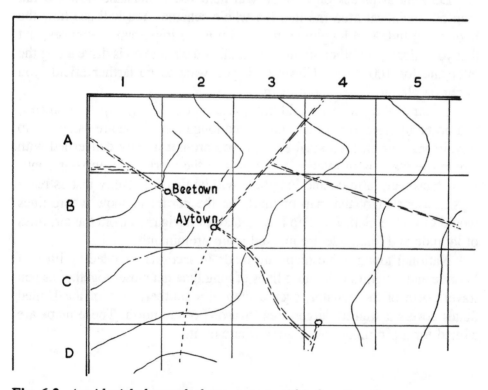

Fig. 6-2. *A grid might be marked on a map to aid in locating places.*

exactly spotting locations in populated areas. The grid squares will be a definite scale size, possibly 1 square kilometer. The system will run over a large area, so it might cover several maps, depending on the scale, and numbers on your map might already be quite high—running from lowest to highest both ways from the bottom left corner of the first sheet.

Letters are not used in this system, so the numbers both ways have to be read in a certain sequence or you get the wrong result. Those numbers across the map are read before the numbers up the sides. One way of remembering the sequence is that you go along the passage before you go up the stairs. Besides the square numbers, another one is added to indicate tenths of a square, so you have three figures in each direction. Suppose you estimate a place is 4/10 of a square past line 27. The reading that way is then 274. Suppose you estimate a place is 6/10 past the line numbered 18 horizontally and 4/10 past the line numbered 21 vertically (FIG. 6-3A). The grid reference is described in two groups of three figures, so the place is 186 214. Remember to quote the horizontal figures before the vertical figures. Always use three figures, even if one is zero. If a place is located exactly at crossing lines (FIG. 6-3B), the reference would be 240 230.

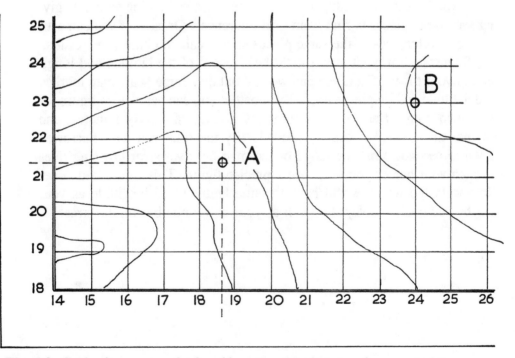

Fig. 6-3. *Grid references can be found by estimating distances from marked lines.*

For most purposes, estimating tenths of a square is sufficient. You can use a scale divided into tenths of a scale kilometer for greater precision. A little square scale marked both ways, called a *roamer* or a *template* measures exact locations, but estimating gets very close. If a square is 1 kilometer (about 5/8 mile) on each side, 1/10 of this distance brings you within 100 meters (just over 300 feet), so you would be within shouting distance!

An index of place names can look rather formidable, particularly if it is of the whole United States, such as in an atlas. If it is an atlas of the whole country, the index will be divided into states. The page numbers of the map or maps covering each state will be listed at the start of the state entry. Towns and other places in the alphabetical index will then have a letter and number to show which square contains the place. You find the page and the square on it, and a little searching inside the square should lead you to the town.

You can get some fun out of finding places if you work with a friend. One of you can search the index and the other find the places, then switch. You can search for towns of the same name in different states. Some are repeated frequently because immigrants often named the places they settled after the place they came from in Europe.

If you have a map with grid squares, practice estimating tenths by giving each other places to find from grid references. Or each of you can estimate grid references of the same places so you can compare your results.

Somewhere in your area should be a record of the latitude and longitude of your town. If not, you can work it out on a large-scale map marked with latitude and longitude lines. Even better, you can get a close figure for your own home. Remember degrees are divided into sixty minutes, and minutes are divided into sixty seconds. By the time you have narrowed down to seconds along the edge of the map both ways for crossing lines through your home, you will have a precise figure. This figure is unique. No one in the whole world has the same latitude and longitude as you. Maybe you could display it as well as your house number on the street!

7

Road Maps

Highway or *ROAD MAPS* ARE THE BEST-KNOWN AND MOST-USED maps. Most of them are intended to help a motorist get from point A to point B as quickly as possible. Usually the emphasis is on primary routes with little information on lesser roads and not much notice taken of rivers, railroads, and minor townships. Not all road maps are like that, but if you want to have a long distance on one sheet of paper, you must expect to lose much detail. A map showing how to drive from coast to coast of the United States has to be at a scale of about 100 miles to 1 inch, so you cannot expect much except main highways, state borders, and large towns.

As scales get bigger, you can expect information on more roads and more information about all types of roads. Many state maps are to a scale large enough that all roads, except the most minor ones, are shown. Such maps, officially published by the state authorities, are usually the most comprehensive, but gas station maps might be good alternatives. Some atlases covering all or part of the country manage to pack in a surprising amount of motoring information using the largest scales that state areas and page sizes will allow. If you want to know about every road in a small locality, you can find the information on one of the largest-scale topographical survey maps.

Any map is worth having, but you cannot trust them all. A free map might be more concerned with advertising than the accuracy of all details on the map. A map might have symbols stamped on it show tourist attractions, campgrounds, or other features. Not all of these maps can be trusted for other information. Be careful of old maps. The date of the last revision should be marked on it. A new highway might have sprawled across the area or some alterations to the road system might have been made since the map was published.

Scales

Road maps are drawn to many different scales. In most cases the mapmaker tries to give you as much map as possible on a given size paper. If the mapmaker puts a map of Rhode Island on the same size paper as one of Texas, he or she can use a much larger scale for the first. Loose maps have to be a size that is convenient to handle, even if they are kept partially folded. Scales are more of a problem in atlases, where each state is on one or two pages of a set size and scales must vary from page to page. For instance, in a Rand McNally atlas of road maps, Texas is spread across two pages at 30 miles per inch, while both New Hampshire and Vermont are on one page at 16 miles per inch.

You usually look at a road map to find out distances, so it is important to first check the scale. You might find one or more scales in the margin similar to those on topographic survey maps (FIG. 2-4). More likely, the scale will be simpler and smaller. On some maps it is just a line with a distance (FIG. 7-1A). A better scale might still be short, but with a few divisions (FIG. 7-1B), or it might also show metric distances (FIG. 7-1C). A more useful way of showing the scale is to include it in one or more sides of the

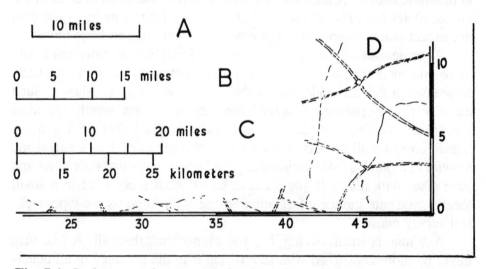

Fig. 7-1. *Scales on road maps might be shown in several ways, including around the map border.*

border (FIG. 7-1D). This kind of scale allows you to check much greater distances without having to repeat the short scale many times to get a total.

Most people think in inches. You can look at two places on the map and estimate that they are 5 inches apart. When you put a rule against the scale, you find the short line representing 25 miles is actually 5/8 inch long. That is easy to convert: 5 miles is represented by 1/8 inch and 1 inch represents 40 miles, so the two places are about 200 miles apart. Scales are not always this easy to convert, but you usually can estimate the number of miles per inch on the map. Another way to measure distance is to mark the scale length along the edge of a piece of paper and repeat it as often as necessary to cover the distance you need.

Scale might be related to population density. Where more people live, you find more roads. If most of the people in a state live in one part, you might find that part drawn to a larger scale. Within that part you might find town plans to an even larger scale, while the thinly populated part is on a small scale. Be careful not to confuse the scales as you switch from one map to another.

On many road maps, distances are shown between marked points along important roads. The legend can tell you how these distances are noted. You can add the distances shown and get a total without referring to a scale.

Elevations

A highway map is just that. You have to remember its main purpose is to show roads and the places they connect. If it has a large scale, it might show details of places of interest, state and national parks, county boundaries, and lakes. It might not mention rivers and railroads. The main thing lacking on highway maps is an indication of heights. If the map shows a mountain range, it might be named, along with spot elevations of peaks, but no contour lines or guide to the ups and downs of roads is shown.

The mapmaker assumes that a modern automobile can travel any road on the map without difficulty. That might be so, but knowing something about gradients might be helpful, if only so you are warned of a long drag uphill where you could be delayed by slow-moving trucks. If you look at most road maps, the impression you get is that the land shown is flat. It might be, but usually heights vary widely. Take, for example, the state of Virginia, which ranges from sea level to 5729 feet at the top of Mount Rogers. Many variations in height between these figures must occur all over the state, but a highway map does not give you many clues to where they are.

You can learn something about heights, even if no contour lines guide you. If the roads shown are almost straight, the land is fairly flat. Winding road might have been built around higher or lower ground and will probably move up and down themselves, but not always, because they might just go around private property or places of special interest. If you are looking at a freeway on a map, it will not rise and fall very much, but if it winds about, it is avoiding deeper valleys or higher hills. If a spot elevation on a peak is given, you can assume the land around it is high, since the peak will not just shoot upwards from a plain.

Names might help. The name of a mountain range will be given along the line of the highest parts, even if the map has no shading or other indication of height. "Blue Ridge Parkway" tells you the road follows a high ridge. If a place name includes "gap," "summit," or "pass" in its name, it will be high.

Water in a lake is level, so a road skirting a lake should be generally level, although it might go over some short hills. If a river is shown, discover its direction. It will be falling all the way, so any road near it will also be going from high to low ground. A road following the coast might be level, but it might climb alongside cliffs.

If you can examine a physical map before following a highway map, it will give you an idea of the levels you will encounter. It need not be to the same scale as the highway map and could be part of a school atlas.

Highways

The most prominent features of a highway map are the roads. They must show up against other features. All roads are not the same, so the mapmaker indicates their types by the way they are drawn. How the different roads are shown depends on the scale and how many colors are available. On a black-and-white map, a few different types of line and spacing can be used, but with colors it is possible to provide a wide range of information about roads.

Freeways are most prominent, with toll roads almost as prominent. Your eye is drawn to these roads immediately. The colors used depend on the map publishers, but some examples are shown in FIG. 7-2A. Other four-lane highway are also shown clearly. All of these are roads needed by anyone looking for through routes. They are drawn with color between dark lines. Lesser roads are usually a color without border lines. Red is common. The width of line indicates the status of the road (FIG. 7-2B). Farther down the scale might be roads colored grey or brown or uncolored parallel

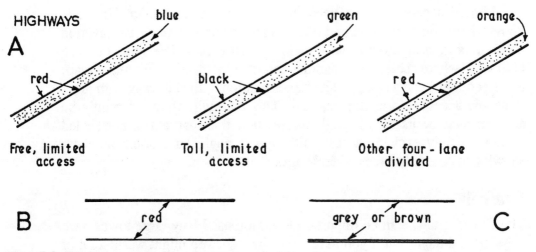

Fig. 7-2. *Highways on a map often are marked in color.*

lines (FIG. 7-2C). Not every map uses the same methods of marking roads, so examine the legend before planning a route on the map.

Many roads are numbered; their numbers are the best way to identify them on the ground and on the map. Map symbols give the number surrounded by a shape similar to that used on markers beside the actual road. It might be a fairly exact reproduction, if the scale is large enough, or a simplified pattern with little or no color, on a small scale. An interstate highway will certainly be marked (FIG. 7-3A). U.S. road numbers appear inside some sort of shield (FIG. 7-3B). Other roads have simpler symbols (FIG. 7-3C). If your map takes you over the Canadian or Mexican border, look for those countries' special symbols on roads.

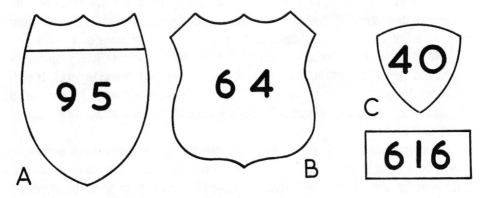

Fig. 7-3. *Road identification symbols on a map might be drawn to look similar to actual road markers.*

Limited-access highways need special treatment on a map. You must know where you can get on and off. A small white square over a junction on an important highway usually indicates full access. For some of these highways, where access information cannot be included on the main map, an inset might show a straight-line representation of the highway with junctions and access information marked. This map will almost certainly be accompanied by its own legend. Remember, this diagram is not scaled because it only explains access, although it might have some numbers showing distances between interchanges.

Symbols

The size of a town can be important to motorists. Many large towns have ways around them, but if you have to go through, you might waste a lot of time in congested traffic. If the scale allows and the town is large enough, the outline of the town might be shown, probably in brown shading. If the scale is smaller or the town is not very large, it appears just a dot. On some maps, dots of different sizes are used to show the size of a town. The size of type used for the name of a town also indicates its size. On some road and state maps, towns are shown as open circles with a mark inside that indicates the population. These symbols vary between maps and you should check the legend, but some examples are shown in FIG. 7-4A.

Other symbols on a highway map depend on the features of a state. A state with plenty of recreational facilities will have suitable symbols on its maps. A tree might represent a state park (FIG. 7-4B). Airports are marked with the outline of an airplane, with different shapes for different types (FIG. 7-4C). National parks are too big for symbols; their shapes are usually shown in green. On a larger-scale inset map, look for its own legend because some symbols might not be the same. Symbols with numbers often refer to a list of civic buildings, museums, and other places of interest.

Most states have welcome stations just inside their borders on interstates and other important roads. Look for the symbol in the legend. It will probably be a colored star or triangle in a circle (FIG. 7-4D). If you call a visitors' station, you can probably get a state map as well as some specialty maps and town plans.

One symbol that is sometimes difficult to find is a compass arrow. It might be a simple arrow or it might be in the form of a badge or emblem, with N at the top. Your map might not have any indication of north. Assume the top of the map is north, unless a prominent indication states otherwise.

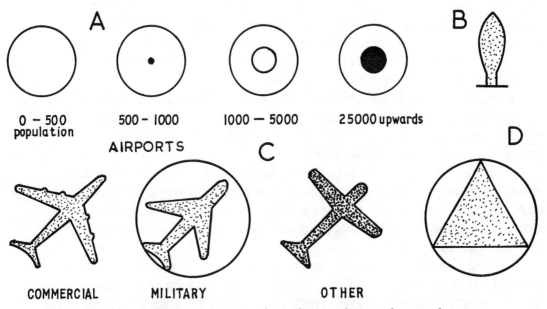

A

| 0 – 500 population | 500 – 1000 | 1000 – 5000 | 25000 upwards |

B

AIRPORTS

C

| COMMERCIAL | MILITARY | OTHER |

D

Fig. 7-4. *Symbols have different meanings, depending on the way they are drawn.*

Before using a highway map as a guide to going somewhere, get to know all it has to offer. Learn the symbols. Become used to the scale so that you can estimate distances. Find out the sizes of towns. Look for clues to heights. With a friend, you can test each other on such things as the number of airports in the state, how many roads go under the interstate, which is the biggest town between point A and point B, and what numbered roads you should take to get from point C to point D. The map will almost certainly have grids with letters and numbers. Ask each other to find places in particular squares. Find which square has the most towns.

Somewhere on the map might be a table of distances between the larger places on the map. These tables are not all arranged in the same way, but a common chart arrangement has a grid of squares with figures in them. You look for the name of one town at the side and look across the squares until you come under the name of the other town across the top. The figure in the square where your lines cross is the distance between the towns in miles.

Simple Routes

The highway map is intended to help you find your way in some sort of vehicle. The differences in types of road will affect your journey. You might consider using some very minor roads in a compact car, but you would not choose to go that way in a large truck or a big motor home, unless you had no alternative. If you study the legend and check the types of road, you can see where better roads might add to the distance, but offer faster travel because of their better condition.

Your ability to read maps allows you to suit your intentions as well as the vehicle. You do not always want to go directly to your destination. You might take some interesting side trips or divert to a town where you can buy groceries or find lodging for the night.

Even if all you want to do is to get somewhere in a reasonable amount of time, without side trips, and the route is obviously a single road, advance study of the map will tell you such things as the overall distance, probable travel time, suitable stopping places for rest or fuel, and when you can expect to reach them.

Suppose you have arranged to pick up a friend early in the morning at Adams Field Airport in Little Rock, Arkansas, then pick up another passenger at Forrest City, and take them both to Memphis. The map shows you that you should use the I-40 interstate and the total distance will be about 150 miles (FIG. 7-5). You will be traveling east in the morning, so if the sun is shining, you will need to wear sunglasses. You notice that U.S. 70 is almost parallel with the interstate and that Forrest City on it. You see a rest area about 60 miles from your start and another at about 90 miles. You might not need them, but you know they are available.

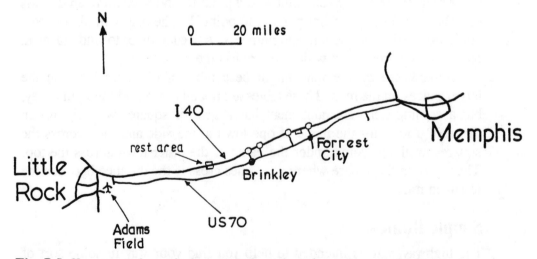

Fig. 7-5. *You can work out the best route from the information on a highway map.*

To reach Forrest City, you could pass the second rest area and take the next interchange, or you could leave at any of several earlier interchanges and go into Forrest City on U.S. 70. If you know where your second passenger lives, that might influence which way you go. At an average speed of 50 miles per hour, the whole journey should take about 3 hours. Will it? Overestimating speed on a journey is easy to do. Allow a little longer. You might run into a lot of traffic at the airport or in the streets of Memphis.

Difficult Routes

In the previous example, the route between two places is simple because an almost-straight highway connects them. For many journeys, particularly if you must cross a pattern of roads going the other way, planning a route is not so simple. Plenty of roads might be available, but perhaps none of them go far enough in the right direction.

Check possible roads on the map. Some might be unsuitable for your vehicle. You might not want to use a gravel road in any case. What about hills? If the map indicates hills, you might want to choose a longer, flatter road than one that is very hilly. If towns lie along some roads, you might want to go another way to avoid congestion. Or perhaps, out of interest, you prefer to go through towns. The shortest route in mileage is not necessarily the shortest one in time. If time is important, and a freeway covers most of the journey, adding many miles to join and leave it might be worthwhile, so that you benefit by the constant speed you drive on it. A great many considerations need to be weighed, and a map can help you see what route will be best in a particular circumstance.

Suppose you want to find the shortest way through a collection of roads, none of which go far in the right direction, but all of which seem to be of equal merit. Start by drawing a straight line on the map between your intended start and finish, using a soft pencil so that you can erase it. This line will show you roads that are near the shortest direction (FIG. 7-6A). You must start by using a road some way off the direct route (FIG. 7-6B). When you come to a junction where the map shows you ought to turn, pencil another straight line from there to the destination (FIG. 7-6C). That line is your new direct route. Find the road that appears to take you nearest to the new line and follow that until you need to change direction again. Draw a line from this new point (FIG. 7-6D) and find another road going as near as possible in the right direction. Continue this method, adding more lines until you get to your final destination on the map. You can check distances

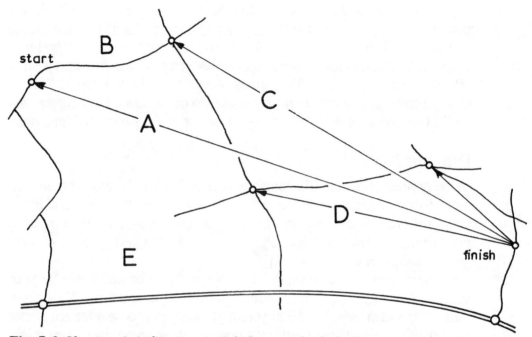

Fig. 7-6. *If a route is indirect, you might have to check the best way to go each time you need to change direction.*

this way and compare the total, as well as possible travel time, with going a longer way to use a freeway (FIG. 7-6E).

If you want to plan a journey that will take several days by car, use a small-scale map that covers the whole distance. You might see more than one suitable route. Compare the rates, taking into account scenery, quality of roads, places of interest, available accommodations, and your personal interests. If you will be making the return journey, you might go one way and come back another. Estimate daily distances and look for possible stopping places.

If you will be using just freeways, that small-scale map might be all you need. Usually, large-scale maps of parts of the route are good to have for the extra information they contain. You might need town plans. If you will be crossing state lines, look for welcome stations. They can provide you with up-to-date state maps and plans of the larger towns. Check these against the maps you already have and note any changes.

Using Many Maps

Be careful when using several maps. The small-scale map might show 40 miles to 1 inch. The large-scale map might be at a scale of 10 miles to 1 inch, or for an interesting part, the scale might be 4 miles to 1 inch. Confusing distances is easy when you move from one map to another. It is even easier when you use town plans. A town may be mapped at 2 inches to 1 mile. In a car, even at town speeds, you might cover 1 inch on the map while you are glancing down at it!

If you are the navigator in a car, think of yourself as being in a similar position to that of a navigator on a ship or airplane. A navigator aims to know where he or she is at all times. Keep a note of odometer readings. If you have any doubt, you will know the distance from the last check. Have a rule and a pair of dividers with you, as well as a soft pencil. Keep a constant check on landmarks, road crossings, townships, and anything else you can match on the ground and the map.

You might not need a compass very often, but taking one along is a good idea. If visibility is decreased by fog, intense darkness, or heavy rain, the compass can help you decide what to do at a fork with no visible sign or at some other awkward point in your journey.

Collect road maps and keep them for future reference. If you travel long distances for vacation or other reasons, pick up maps when you can at gas stations and welcome stations. Visit local information centers. They might give you maps of their localities that have more detail than any other maps. National and state parks all have their own maps. Some commercially run enterprises issue maps. If you obtain maps that appear to overlap on areas, you might find features on one map that can supplement information on another. You might be able to cross-check possible errors.

If you keep maps for a long time or are given old ones, check the revision dates. Changes in roads might have been made since the publication date. New highways are always being built. Developments may cause routes to be altered. Road numbers may change. An old map might still be correct, but it needs checking. Get an up-to-date version if you can. The date of publication or the date of the last revision can usually be found somewhere in the map margin.

8

Away from Roads

ONE OF THE MOST INTERESTING AND ENJOYABLE WAYS TO USE MAPS and compasses is to take them on an expedition into wild country that might be open or wooded, but with little or no sign of use by people. You have to find your way without any road signs to help you. You really are an explorer. Natural features will be your guides, rather than roads, towns, houses, or any other man-made landmark. Before going into wild country, you should practice the map and compass work you will use so that you have no doubts about finding your way.

You might not have any large tracts of unspoiled country near you, but you can use the same methods of finding your way in small areas. This kind of exploration might be scaled down, but it will give you practice that might be of use to you if at some time you are able to go into a wilderness area. Of course, being able to use a map and compass efficiently is important before you go into country where you have a very real chance of getting lost. You can learn the skills you need almost anywhere, and then you can tackle exploring seriously with the certainty that you will succeed or be able to solve any problems. Do not go straight into the wilds alone hoping to learn how to use the map and compass as you progress.

When you are traveling by road, on some occasions you might find a use for a compass, but most of the time you can manage with the map alone. If you start exploring undeveloped country, a compass and the ability to use it become important. With few man-made signs to help you, compass bearings related to the map might be all you have to show you the way, whether you are walking or riding a horse. When canoeing, you know you are on a river, but you might have to identify which part. If you are crossing a lake, the compass is necessary for navigation.

In this sort of map and compass work, you are dependent on your own resources. If you get lost, you cannot ask a passing motorist the way.

Good explorers do not travel alone. Companionship is important, but besides that, sharing equipment has practical advantages. You have help in case of an accident. For map and compass work, you can share decisions. If two or more people plot a route and agree, you have confirmation. If you can make your first expeditions with an experienced companion, you will learn a lot. Advanced training and practice are important, but coping with route finding in a remote place is the final test.

Maps

A motorist's map is not much use to you if you are going into wild country. It might help you to get there, and it will show you roads and other man-made features around the chosen undeveloped area. You might be glad of these features to confirm your course plotting. You might not be able to get away from aircraft. If your road map shows the location of one or more airports, the flights of aircraft might indicate directions.

State maps might not be much more use than road maps, even if they include back country in their area. Details of those parts on a state map might not be enough for safe and accurate exploring. Some national and state parks have maps intended for exploring visitors, but you will probably be following marked trails, which can be worthwhile and enjoyable, but does not depend on your skills with a map and compass.

If you are going into the wild, you will need topographic maps. How many and what scales depends on several factors. You get the most details on maps of large scale, but if it is a large scale, not much land is represented on one piece of paper, so you would need to carry a great many maps if you intended to travel far. You might need the largest scale available for local details, but you might find all you want on fewer small-scale maps if you will be traveling for several days.

Topographic maps, which can also be called *quadrangle maps*, are bounded by lines of latitude and longitude. The maps you probably will find the most useful are the 7½-minute series national topographic maps. They have a scale of 1:24,000; 1 inch on the map represents 2000 feet on the ground. The area included measures 7½-minute latitude north to south and 7½-minute longitude east to west. Each map covers about 8 miles each way and gives the greatest detail available. Some maps are available that are twice as wide with a slightly different scale and give double the width of coverage.

Next are the 15-minute series, to a scale of 1:62,500 . On these maps, 1 inch represents nearly 1 mile. The area covered on each sheet is about 20 miles each way, or more than four times as much as a 7^1/2-minute sheet. A 15-minute map probably will carry all the information you need and reduce the number of maps you have to take. In wild country, you are unlikely to walk 20 miles a day in a straight line, so a few of these maps should cover expeditions of several days. You should have maps of every bit of ground you expect to travel. Don't think that if at one point you expect to go over the edge of the map and come back a little farther on, you don't need to bother with another map. You might run into an unexpected hazard that another map would have shown.

A map supplier has index sheets of topographic and other maps. Select sufficient maps from the index to be certain that you cover all the territory you expect to travel. If you will keep much of your exploration to a small area, you might select one or more 7^1/2-minute maps to cover that area and rely on 15-minute maps for the rest of the trip.

Compasses

Any of the types of compass described in chapter 4 will be useful in wilderness travel, but you need to be able to sight with reasonable accuracy. A sighting compass allows you to read the bearings directly, but the Silva compass or another type where you can look across the compass and set to find the angle, should give you sufficient accuracy. Much depends on the country. If you want to set a map with a compass to match hills, clumps of trees, and other prominent landmarks, extreme accuracy is not so important, but if you are in a flat desert with only a few small features, a course must be plotted with more accuracy.

Your party should always carry more than one compass, in case one gets lost or damaged. The second one need not be as good as the one normally used, but it must be more than a toy. A cord around your neck is a good way of securing a compass, but do not let it swing. It is better off in a shirt pocket or tucked inside your shirt. It might be fitted into a protective case, but you want it to be accessible, so don't pack it away too tightly.

When canoeing, you can secure your compass on a *thwart* or in the bottom of the canoe. You can check quickly the direction you are going, which helps identify the part of the river you are on, since some twist a surprising amount. If you are crossing a lake, the compass helps you keep to the course you have planned.

Compass Walks

When traveling in the wilderness, you must try to keep as close as possible to the course you have planned. You might see some landmark you can use, but if you have to depend on the compass, you must practice ahead of time. You need to give yourself plenty of practice without going far from home. Any open space of moderate size, such as a field or a town park, can be used.

A simple test is to try to walk a triangular course so that you finish where you started. Mark a starting point with a stone on the ground. Set the compass to north. Walk with your compass in that direction (FIG. 8-1A) any convenient number of steps, say 25 or 50. Set the compass to 120° and walk the same number of steps in that direction (FIG. 8-1B). At that point, set the compass to 240° and walk that direction (FIG. 8-1C). If you have navigated correctly, you will arrive back at the starting point, having traveled around a triangle with equal sides. You probably won't work exactly, because paces vary and following a compass within a few degrees while walking is difficult. Keep trying. Make it a competition with the friends who will come with you on a real expedition.

Put a pole, or something else you can see from a distance, at your starting point. Follow a course north a number of paces (FIG. 8-1D). The further you go, the more difficult the test becomes. Go east from that point the same distance (FIG. 8-1E). Now sight the starting pole across your compass. It should be southwest, but allow yourself and others a margin of error (FIG. 8-1F). See who can get the bearing closest.

Bearings are not usually simple directions in the wild, and you must be prepared to work with various angles. Try starting with any angle, possibly one that best fits into the field where you practice. In the next example, start with a bearing of 120° (FIG. 8-1G). Add 90° to it at your turning point (FIG. 8-1H). After walking the same distance, sight the starting pole. It ought to be at 345° (FIG. 8-1J). This exercise should be no more difficult than the previous test, but because you are working with degrees, not directions, you need more concentration.

A simple test of your ability to follow a route is to walk on a bearing, then turn and take a bearing of your starting point. This second bearing is called a *reciprocal bearing* (FIG. 8-1K) and should be 180° more or less than your first bearing. If the first bearing is less than 180°, add 180° to

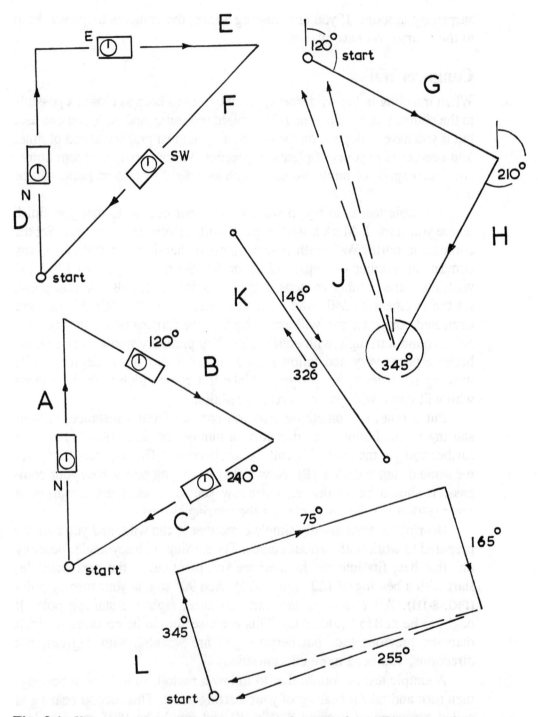

Fig. 8-1. *You can practice following compass bearings by walking around set courses.*

check the reciprocal. If it is more than 180°, subtract 180°. Try this test at increasing distances to see how close you or your friends can hold to a course. Taking a reciprocal bearing is a useful test on triangular or other courses. When you get into the wild, it is a good way of checking your progress, particularly if you can see something easily at your starting point and your destination is out of sight.

You can try a square or rectangular course (FIG. 8-1L). The larger this course is, the more difficulty you will have getting your final sights accurate. Keep trying. Notice that the bearings of opposite sides are reciprocals of each other.

A further step is to lay out to scale on paper, with a rule and protractor, a course with several legs of different lengths and bearings. Get your friends to compete on a scaled-up version on the ground. Paces vary, so with several bearings and distances, you must not expect too close a result. If competitors get within 10°, they are doing well.

All of this practice is related to orienteering (see chapter 10). Orienteering is good training for wilderness travel.

Something else you need to be able to do before going into forests or wilderness country with your map and compass is read bearings from the map and transfer them to a route on the ground or take bearings on the ground and transfer them to the map. You should know where you are and where you are going, both in fact on the ground and to scale on the map. You might have periods when you are uncertain, but they should be brief if you are a good navigator. You can practice almost anywhere, without going into the wild. Try it in a small area, then increase the distances. Roads and houses don't matter, as long as you interpret directions on the map and ground with your compass. Also try to use an area with trees or undergrowth that you can pass through without being able to see very far ahead.

Choose a simple route to something you can see that is marked on the map. It could be a group of trees. When you look at the map, several groups of trees might be marked. You might identify your chosen group by estimating its distance or comparing the spacing of the groups. Or you might orient your map with your compass so it is set to match the ground, then sight across it over the marked starting point. Your line of sight will go through your marked group of trees (FIG. 8-2A).

Another way to choose a route is to take a bearing of the trees with your compass. Suppose the bearing is 62° and you are using a Silva, or similar, compass (FIG. 8-2B). Lightly pencil a north-south line through your starting point on the map (FIG. 8-2C). Use the compass as a protractor on

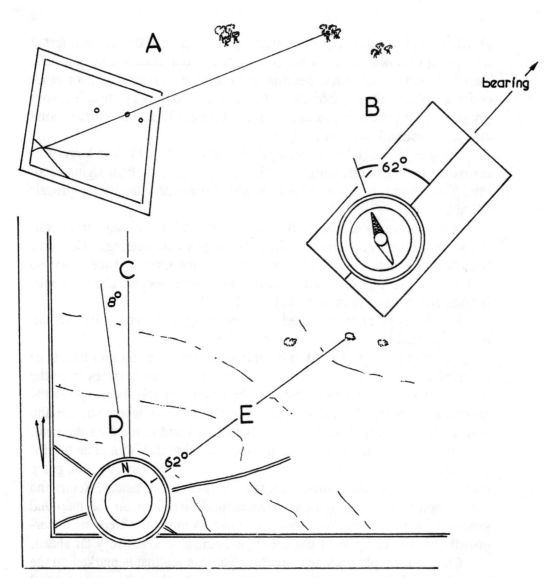

Fig. 8-2. *You can obtain a bearing from a sight line on a map by using your compass.*

the map. You can keep it at the bearing setting. Check the amount of declination from the arrows in the margin. In the example, it is 8° west. Put the compass over the starting point with its north marked 8° west of the pencil line (FIG. 8-2D). The bearing line on the base or the 60″ mark on the rim will point at the group of trees (FIG. 8-2E) on the map. You can reverse the process to find a bearing on the map and transfer it to the direction on the ground.

Hidden Destinations

Arranging a route becomes a little more difficult if you cannot see your destination. It might be out of sight nearly all the way, or it could be hidden when you pass through trees or cross a valley. You have to trust your compass.

For practice, find a local heavily wooded area or an area with some mixed undergrowth that you can pass through without seeing far ahead. From you map, locate a starting point that you can identify on the ground. Look for something on the other side of the trees or undergrowth that you will recognize when you get there. It might be a meeting of two trails. Draw a light line between your start and finish (FIG. 8-3A).

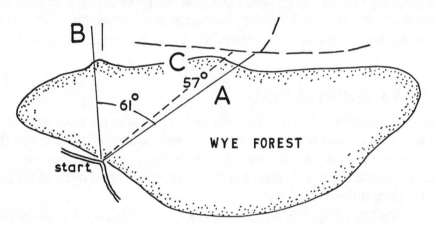

Fig. 8-3. *Where you cannot see far ahead on a bearing, you might follow an offset course.*

Measure or estimate the length of the line so that you will be able to estimate your progress when you walk the route. Find the bearing of this line on your map. Allow for declination (FIG. 8-3B). In theory, if you walk on that bearing (61 ° in the example) long enough, you will come out of the trees exactly at the meeting of the two trails. When you start walking, you will soon discover practical problems. Try to keep on the bearing. If you come to something you must walk around, try to come back the same amount at the other side of it and continue following the bearing. Much depends on the density of trees or other obstructions, but this experiment in following a blind route will show you what problems you might have in the wilderness. If the distance is about 2 miles, and you arrive within 1/4 mile of your intended point, you have done quite well. Practice will help you improve.

In this example, you might get through and not know if you are to the left or right of the trail junction and waste time searching in both directions for it. You can deliberately *aim off* or *offset* your route, changing it to 57° in the example (FIG. 8-3C). If a trail, road, fence, or other easily recognized feature runs near your target point, aim to hit it to one side of the destination. When you get to the feature, you know which way to turn to find the point you want, even if you have made some minor errors while passing through the trees.

Try depending on a compass as much as possible, even when you can find the way with landmarks. The ability to read a compass and rely on it is often essential when traveling in wilder country. You might set out to travel to a place high enough to be seen from your start, but perhaps a valley lies in between. You can work by sight as long as you can see the other end of the route, but change to the compass while you are hidden from it in the valley.

Other Navigation Methods

If you are canoeing, you have no choice but to go where the river takes you. Do your best to read where you are from the bearings of the twists in the river and the drawing on the map. You might think the river flows east. Its general direction might be east, but the direction of some of its loops and twists might surprise you (FIG. 8-4A).

To practice navigating a canoe across a large lake, try a scaled-down crossing of a swimming pool. Mark a start and a finish and take a compass bearing between them (FIG. 8-4B). Float your compass on a piece of wood or a model boat. Swim and push the float while looking only at the compass. Do your best to maintain your course (FIG. 8-4C) and see how close you come to the intended destination—without cheating!

Another skill that might come in handy in the wild is *dead reckoning*, which is also used at sea. You might find it valuable if you are without landmarks or if you want to check a position found by other means. If you go in a certain direction at a certain speed for a certain time, you should know where you are. Variables will affect the result, but dead reckoning gives you a good idea of your current position in relation to your last known position. Suppose you travel southwest for two hours while walking at 3 miles per hour. You should have gone 6 miles in that direction (FIG. 8-5A). Much depends on your skill at estimating walking speed and your ability to stay on course. Mark where you think you are on the map. If a landmark is within view, its bearing will give you a crossing line (FIG. 8-5B). You might

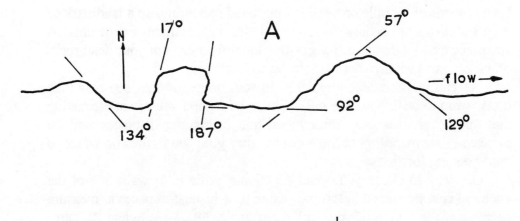

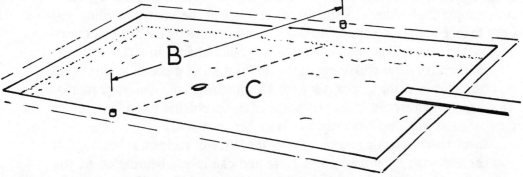

Fig. 8-4. *Bearings taken on a river (A) help you check where you are. You can practice following a bearing on water in a swimming pool (B and C).*

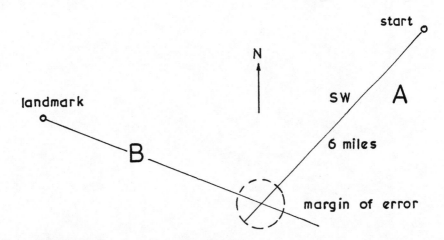

Fig. 8-5. *An estimated distance and route (A) allows you to get your position by checking a bearing (B) on a landmark.*

have an error of $1/4$ mile or more in your dead reckoning, so a landmark or even variations in height shown by contours will confirm your results. A stream or trail might seem like positive identification, but your dead reckoning can put you anywhere within $1/2$ mile along it.

You can practice dead reckoning on your home ground. See how long it takes you to walk a known mile. Check how good you are at estimating that and other distances. Both speed and estimating distances will be affected by surroundings in the wild, but they give you figures on which to base your explorations.

One way to check your dead reckoning skills is to walk one of the enclosed courses shown in FIG. 8-1, using time instead of paces to measure each leg of the course. If you walk the triangle (FIG. 8-1A, B, and C), carefully timing each side, you should arrive back at the start, providing you keep to time and the compass bearings. Longer times on each leg increases your risk of error. The same applies to the other shapes in FIG. 8-1.

You can try dead reckoning in the dark on a flat piece of ground with no obstructions, using a compass with a luminous needle and other marks. This experiment would show you some of the problems faced by a sea or air navigator who depends only on his or her own skill.

In all your navigating, do not forget the value of reciprocal bearings. If you can see where you have come from and can take a bearing on it, you have an immediate check on your course. If it is not 180° different from the course bearing, you are wandering. You might go out of sight of the starting point as you cross a valley, then be able to see it again at the other side. If the reciprocal bearing is off, you will have to correct your course.

9

Into the Wilderness

VERY LITTLE LAND IN THIS COUNTRY, OR IN THE WORLD, HAS NOT been visited by someone before you. In some places, people have looked for gold or other minerals and then abandoned their search. In other places, people have trapped animals and might still do so. Large areas have so far resisted development, whether building, mining, or tree felling. Many areas are protected as national or other parks. Compared with some other countries of the world, the United States is fortunate in having many large undeveloped and only slightly explored tracts of land as well as parts which have been developed as much as any place on earth.

You can find undeveloped land that has seen so little of humans that you can regard it as wilderness. If you look at a map or travel through such an area, you might find an abandoned cabin, evidence of a man-made trail, discarded mine workings, or parts where trees have been felled, but most of the area will still be as nature planned it.

Many of these areas are large and you can travel through them for days without seeing roads, towns, or other evidence of civilization. Other areas are smaller, and you can pass through in a day or a few hours. Many of these smaller wild areas exist, and you might find one near you. This small area is a good place to make early exploration trips to prepare for a trip in a larger area, which might only be possible during a vacation. If things go wrong, and you get lost in one of these smaller areas, you know that if you keep going in any direction you will get out somewhere within a reasonable time.

Planning

This book is about maps and compasses, not planning expeditions, but remember that where you will be dependent on your own resources for several hours or even days, you must be prepared for whatever happens. You should travel in a group of two or more, sharing equipment and skills. You should be fit and correctly dressed, paying particular attention to footwear. You should have all the food and camping equipment you need. Carry first aid equipment and know how to use it. Most important are your maps and compasses.

The choice of maps and compasses is suggested in chapter 8. Be sure your maps cover everywhere you expect to go, including a possible emergency route out. You should have more than one map of the area, carried by different people, in case one is lost or damaged. The maps can be to different scales. If the large-scale, detailed map that you work from is damaged, you can still find your way with the smaller-scale one otherwise used only for general planning. At least two people should carry a compass.

Part of the fun of a wilderness expedition is in planning ahead. It is important for the enjoyment of the trip as well as your safety. Only a fool would set off into the wilderness without adequate preparation. Get all the maps you will use well ahead of time. Learn all you can from them. First study all the guidance they provide for understanding the map. Look at all the information in the margin. Besides scale and north directions, it should tell you the elevation differences of contour lines. A key or legend should show you the meanings of all symbols. If the map doesn't have a legend, you need a separate sheet of symbols that is published with the series of maps. Knowing the symbols is important. In some cases, slight differences in the way a symbol is drawn can change the meaning.

Water might be as important to you in navigating in the wild as roads are elsewhere. Streams and lakes provide a good way to identify your position. You also will need to know about water for drinking.

From the contour lines, you can see how the ground rises and falls. If possible, compare mapped slopes in the wild with some you know elsewhere to get an idea of steepness. Closeness of contour lines will certainly show you where you might not be able to walk and where you might have to scramble up or slide down if you do not go around.

The map will indicate wooded and open areas. But remember that trees grow. If the date of the map is a few years ago, woodland and the undergrowth or vegetation with it might have spread. This growth is more likely with quick-growing conifer trees than with broad-leafed hardwoods. Open areas might be swampy if they are low, even if they are some distance from actual bodies of water.

Your map might indicate trails. If other people have been where you are going, they could have good reasons for following the route they did. You might want to go the same way.

From all this information, you should be able to picture what the scene looks like when viewed from various places. The heights of ground will tell you if you will see one hill behind another or if it will be hidden. The amount of wooded areas will blend into the hills. The hollows may be valleys with water running through them. A lake might be hidden by surrounding water-loving trees. You will see more from high than low ground, so look for places on the map to use as viewpoints as you survey the land over which you want to travel.

As you study the maps, think of the routes you hope to follow, looking for slopes indicated by contour lines and possible hazards due to undergrowth or marshes. Some wooded parts might be almost impenetrable and you might have to go around. You can expect to cross only small streams easily. If a lake has a stream running out of it, the area might be very marshy.

All this information comes from the map before you get to the country it represents. A surprising amount of information is there for you to extract, but a map cannot tell you everything. Learn all you can from it. Someone has carefully surveyed the land and you should be able to trust that person's findings. However, a mapmaker cannot tell it all, and some of your advanced planning might have to be altered when you get there. You must be flexible in your approach to the expedition. Plan ahead as much as you can, but don't insist on sticking rigidly to the plan if you find that another idea would be better when you arrive. The knowledge you gained in advance will still be valuable.

You must decide how far you hope to go. Even if your expedition will last only a few hours, you need to estimate progress and allow for possible delay. If someone will be meeting you with a car at the far side, do not give them an exact time. Be vague, so you have enough time to complete the journey, or else you could start a panic. If you are going into the wilderness for several days, be flexible about distances. You might need to come out at a certain place at about a certain time, but when you meet actual conditions they may be different from what you expect in advance planning. Try not to need a forced march to complete a schedule. You will be better off overestimating travel time, so that the pleasure of the trip is not spoiled by the need to hurry.

You might think you can walk at three miles per hour, and allow five hours walking time to complete fifteen miles. In rough terrain, you will probably do less than that. Allow for time to stop and look, especially if anyone in your party is interested in flowers, trees, or animals. You could build in time for pauses for photography or sketching. That original estimate of fifteen miles would more likely be ten. Much depends on the country. If you have to scramble up or down, find your way through dense forest, or get across an awkward stream, your progress will be slower. You should not go into the wilderness with the idea of covering the longest possible distance in the shortest possible time. Interest in your surroundings and surmounting obstacles are what you have come for, so allow times and distances accordingly.

Routes

Keeping all these factors in mind, you can get down to advance route planning with a pencil on a map. For a one-day expedition in mainly wooded country, you might decide to look at a stream, go to a hill that should serve as a lookout point, then return to your starting point. Estimate distances and times. Draw lines between the points and work out their bearings. Make a note of these figures on a sketch map (FIG. 9-1A) or beside the lines on the actual map.

Suppose the expedition is to last three days. Decide where you will start and finish. Make a note of places you wish to visit. Check distances between them. Are they possible? Where do you hope to stop each night? You need a dry ,level campsite and access to water. How do such places fit into your planning? You might have to juggle possible routes. You might have to abandon a visit to one or more spots.

You could work on the map surface with a soft pencil and erase lines until you have what you want, but printed lines on the map might confuse you. You might find it better to put a piece of tracing paper over the map and draw on that . You can lift it away and see if daily distances look possible and if you will be able to go where you hoped, without the confusion of map details. When you are satisfied that you have planned as accurately as possible without actually seeing the country, either make a master tracing or draw lines on the map with their bearings marked alongside them (FIG. 9-1B). You might decide to make photocopies of the tracing so that each member of your expedition will know what is planned.

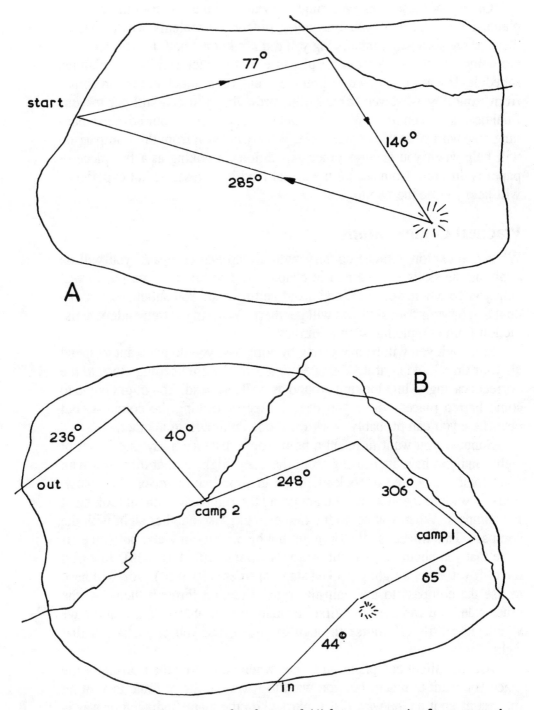

Fig. 9-1. *Following a short route on local ground (A) lets you practice for an extensive expedition (B).*

On any of these trips, you might deviate quite a lot from the original planned route because you encounter practical problems when you get there or see something interesting you did not know about in advance. You are going into the wilderness for pleasure, not to stick rigidly to a planned schedule. If you can plot where you are at any time, much of the fun comes from exploring whatever attracts you, providing you can still get to your final destination on time. When you get home, compare your advance planning map with what you actually did. What you learn from this comparison will help when you arrange other expeditions. Looking at a flat piece of paper is different from seeing the actual land it represents, but experience will help you tie the two together.

Practical Compasswork

When you explore strange country with a map and compass, you will be applying the skills you learned in chapter 8. The practice you put in will help you go where you want and avoid getting lost. You should feel confident that by your own skill you will get there. You can get tremendous satisfaction from completing such a journey.

Although you will be navigating by compass, you do not want to spend all your time looking at it. You need to know you are keeping close to the correct bearings while looking around as well as ahead. You might come to some barren places where you need to keep checking the compass, but elsewhere you can probably work from one landmark to another.

Suppose you want to reach a point some distance away that is out of sight, and you have its bearing from the map. Sight in that direction with your compass. A tree or rock might be in your line of travel (FIG. 9-2A). You can walk to it and know you are going the right way without looking at the compass. When you get to the tree or rock, take another sight with the compass. This time a landmark might not be directly in view, but you estimate that you should aim about 50 yards from a cliff (FIG. 9-2B). Just past the cliff you enter a tightly packed stand of trees (FIG. 9-2C). You will have to use the compass to maintain the right direction through them. At the other side, you can see your first destination (FIG. 9-2D). You might have wandered a little off course through the trees, but you can now put that right.

Another slight complication comes when you know the bearing of the place you want to reach, but you want to leave the direct route to visit an interesting spot on the way. If it is marked on the map, finding your way is easy, but otherwise you will have to estimate. Assuming you can travel

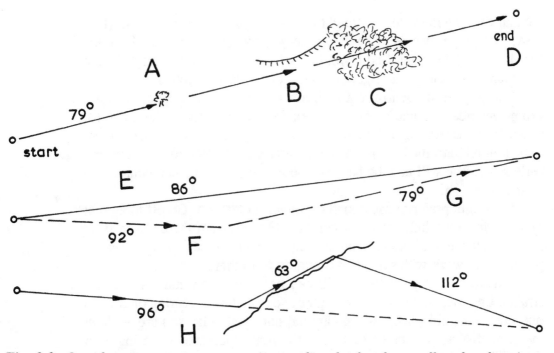

Fig. 9-2. *On a long journey, you can use intermediate landmarks or allow for diversions.*

directly over the ground, note the direct route (FIG. 9-2E). Obtain a bearing of the extra place from the map or by estimation. (FIG. 9-2F). When you get to it, you will have to use another bearing to get to the final point (FIG. 9-2G).

The problem may not always be as simple as that. If the place you want to visit is a fall on a stream, you might be wise to keep to the original route until you meet the stream, then follow it to the fall and get a new bearing from there (FIG. 9-2H).

Obstructions

Wild country is most interesting if it has hills and valleys, with thickly wooded parts as well as some open stretches. It might have animal trails and, possibly, rough roads from past occupation, but otherwise no sign of civilization. This kind of land complicates converting routes on maps to actual journeys on the ground. In many places you cannot arrange to travel far in a straight line.

One problem you might have is dealing with an isolated hill. Suppose the place you are aiming at on the map is the other side of a hill, shown by contour lines on the map. A straight line would take you over the hill (FIG. 9-3A). You might decide to go over it so you can enjoy the view from the top. If you get there and find it would not be worth climbing and decide to go around, you then must figure out how to get back to your route.

One way would be to use a reciprocal bearing, if you expect to see a prominent tree or some other landmark from both sides of the hill (FIG. 9-3B). Note the bearing of it before you start to go around (FIG. 9-3C). Continue around until the bearing of the landmark is the reciprocal of the first (FIG. 9-3D). You will now be back on the original line and can continue to your destination.

You might prefer to use a method shown in FIG. 9-2. Go off to a point that will miss the hill, then follow a new bearing from there. Even if no place beside the hill is marked on the map, you should be able to estimate a position and work with sufficient accuracy from there.

If a prominent peak to the hill can be seen all around, even if the straight-line route does not go through it, you can take a bearing on it from one side of the hill (FIG. 9-3E), go around until you judge you are at about the same distance on the other side of the peak, then take a bearing on it that will be at the same angle to your intended route (FIG. 9-3F) to put yourself back on course.

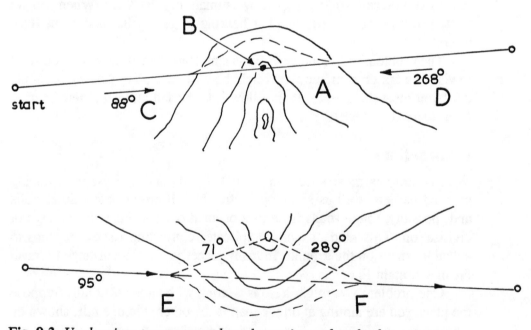

Fig. 9-3. *Use bearings to pass around an obstruction and get back on your route.*

An advantage of being among hills and valleys, trees and open country, and streams and rivers, is that these features are marked on the map. Contours show you rises and falls. A hill that goes to a peak is as good a landmark as a crossroads on a map. Even a hill with a rounded top can serve as a guide. Study the contour lines.

All kinds of water are useful as identifying marks. If you reach a stream, you will have no doubt about the line you are on. Checking its local direction with a compass might allow you to get a close estimate of where you are on the line of the stream on the map (FIG. 9-4A). A more positive spot check will be a bearing of a landmark, such as a hill (FIG. 9-4B). Even better would be a second bearing on another place (FIG. 9-4C). You might not find an exact point for a second bearing, but looking around at the groups of trees might let you picture the arrangement in relation to the stream on your map and on the ground.

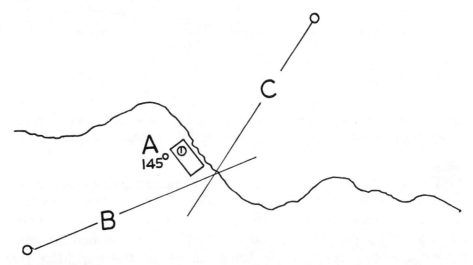

Fig. 9-4. *The direction of a stream (A) will help you fix your position, but bearings on landmarks (B and C) will pinpoint it.*

Correcting Routes

In fairly open country, you usually can keep close to your intended route by referring to the compass and checking landmarks. If a large part of the journey goes through trees or undergrowth, or something else interferes with visibility in all directions, you have more risk of error. This risk increases with distance. Quite often you can find enough landmarks when you reach open ground to make corrections then, but not always.

If the route through trees has breaks where you might see a landmark such as a hilltop, a bearing on that landmark will confirm you are not far off your route (FIG. 9-5A). With the compass bearing you are following, this bearing should give you a fairly close spot check. To be more accurate, you need a second landmark (FIG. 9-5B). The crossing of these sight lines might not be exactly on your dead reckoning line, but it will be a more accurate position.

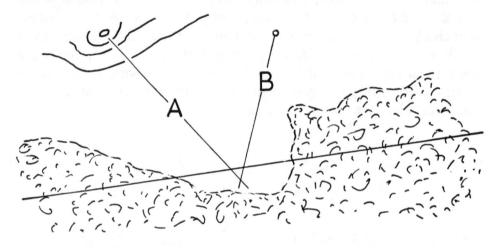

Fig. 9-5. *Once you emerge into the open after following a route with little visibility, you might be able to confirm your position with bearings on landmarks.*

Difficulties arise if you are navigating blind through a forest and have to find a place within the forest, such as a derelict cabin. You have to set a course and estimate distance. If you go directly to it you are lucky or skillful. If you think you have traveled far enough but cannot find the cabin, don't rush around looking for it. You could get lost that way. Mark your position or leave one of your party there. Now go out on compass bearings. If you do not find the cabin, go back to the base point on a reciprocal bearing. Repeat this as often as necessary (FIG. 9-6A).

If what you are aiming for has length, such as a stream, you might allow for errors by using an offset bearing, so that when you reach it you know which way to go to the point you want (FIG. 9-6B). This method is better than aiming directly and arriving at the stream without knowing whether to search upstream or downstream for the point you want. Errors magnify with distance and the number of times you have to correct a course. You cannot keep a straight course through trees, and each time you

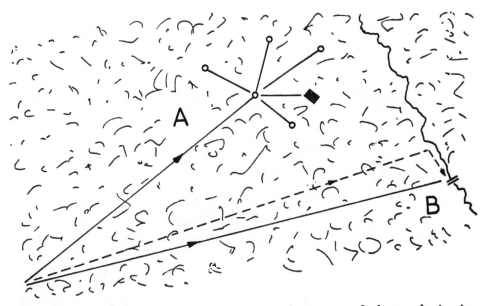

Fig. 9-6. *You might need to search on specific bearings to find your destination (A). Following an offset bearing (B) might be helpful.*

use the compass, you might be slightly to one side or the other of where you think you are. Errors might cancel each other out by chance, but if each error is in the same direction, you could finish quite a distance from your intended destination. So use an offset bearing whenever possible.

Suppose you get lost or are sure of where your are. Think about it calmly. Identify the last known place. Can you take a reciprocal bearing of it? If so, you know what line you are on. If not, consider how long you have traveled from it and in what general direction. Consider the country you have traveled over. Three hours on rough country might have taken you 6 miles. You know the general direction, even if you wandered about. Draw an arc on the map to a scale distance of 6 miles from the last known place, covering the general area you must be in (FIG. 9-7A). It could be a freehand curve. You know that you have not gone outside that arc and must be well within its width, so you already have a good idea of your general position.

Set your map with the compass. See how this compares with the actual land. Look around for places on the ground that should also be on the map. Do you see a valley? It probably will have a stream. You might not see water, but do you see willows or other water-loving trees? What about hills? Can you see an isolated hill or a range of hills? They will help you orient your map and yourself. You might know enough already to continue

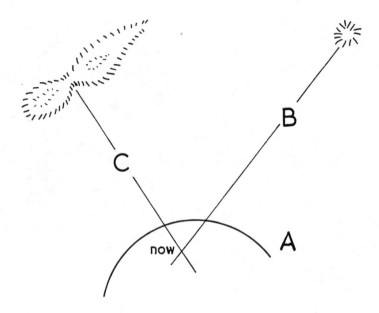

o last known

Fig. 9-7. *When you are unsure of your position, an arc and bearings might give you a fix.*

your journey, but you might be able to pinpoint your position with more accuracy.

A bearing on an isolated hill shown on the map will put you on a line within the arc (FIG. 9-7B). Ideally, find another landmark. That might be too much to expect, but contour lines on the map might match hills you can see, even if they are broad in your view and you cannot sight on an exact spot. You might get a bearing on a high part or a cleft that will give you a crossing line near where you must be (FIG. 9-7C). You are not lost. The farther away that sort of landmark is, the less the risk of error.

Believe your bearings, if you are certain you have identified correctly the landmarks on the ground and on the map. Whenever possible, get a third bearing. If the three cross close together, that area is where you are. If they cross exactly on one spot, that is luck. You might have a tendency to always look ahead, but you might find a good landmark behind you. If possible, use bearing lines at widely spaced angles for the greatest accuracy.

If you have a map and a compass, you are never really lost. Do not panic—look at the problem logically, and use your map and compass skills to solve it.

10

Orienteering

IF YOU WANT TO TEST YOUR SKILLS WITH A MAP AND COMPASS, THE answer might be orienteering. Orienteering is a sport or recreation in which you find your way between various check points across undeveloped country. On an orienteering course, you run against the clock to find control points by using your map and compass skills. Although speed is a factor, the winner is usually the person best able to choose a route from the map and follow it on the ground.

Orienteering can be just a simple event arranged among friends, a regionally organized competition, or even a national or international event. Orienteering has a worldwide following.

Because it is an international sport, you will usually find that orienteering events use metric distances, so "think metric" from the start. It's not so difficult if you remember that 1 meter is about 39 inches. You are unlikely to have to bother with kilometers (1000 meters or about 5/8 mile).

Orienteering started in Scandinavia, where plentiful forest and wild country shows little evidence of human presence. It started as a form of cross-country racing in which competitors found their own way by map. Just after World War II, the name "orienteering" started being used. Interest spread, and now the International Orienteering Federation (IOF) covers more than 20 countries. Divisions of IOF include the United States Orienteering Federation and the Canadian Orienteering Federation. Because of the organization of the sport, many rules and policies are standardized, but local variations do exist. You will have to check with the organizers of particular competitions for details. This chapter is an introduction to usual procedures.

Although any type of compass can be used to guide you around an orienteering course, the Silva type is particularly suitable and is the standard in all competitions. You can practice orienteering with almost any large-scale map, but special maps are prepared for competitions. An orienteering course usually does not cover a very large area, but within that area, a map needs plenty of detail. This detail could be added to a standard map, but for important events special large-scale maps are produced that eliminate unnecessary information and emphasize what competitors need. Many symbols are different from those on standard maps.

Compasses

The basic Silva compass (FIG. 4-3F) has all the features needed for orienteering. Some variations might be a little more suitable for an enthusiast. A large magnifier is useful. Graduations on the rim should be easy to read. You can get a compass with a wider needle. Some compasses are particularly suitable for orienteering at night. If you prefer a compass with a larger or smaller base, you can get one. Most orienteering compasses can hang from a cord around your neck. An unusual one has a band that fits around your thumb. Sighting compasses are more appropriate to long-distance travel than to orienteering.

You will use your compass to get bearings at brief intervals between stretches of running, walking, or scrambling. You want to keep it safe and be able to get at it quickly. Don't let it swing on a neck cord. If you have it on the cord, slip it into a pocket or inside your shirt.

Orienteering maps have a large number of lines across them arranged in the direction of magnetic north and south, so you don't have to bother with declination. Plotting a course is a matter of three simple steps. Draw a line between the start and the destination of a particular leg of the competition (FIG. 10-1A). Put the long edge of the compass base against this line (FIG. 10-1B). Ignore the needle and turn the compass dial until the north mark and the parallel line in the transparent base point to magnetic north on the map. You can probably move the compass base along the course line until the center of the compass comes over one of the north-south lines on the map (FIG. 10-1C).

You could now read the bearing from the figures on the rim, but you usually do not need to do this. Away from the map, hold the compass in

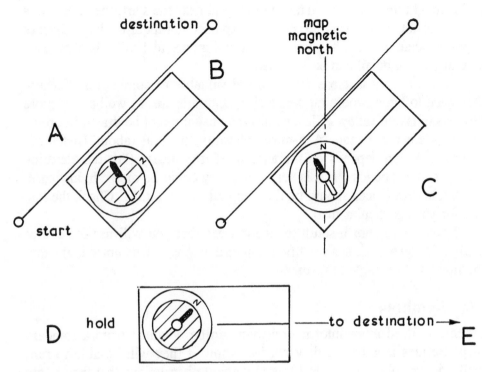

Fig. 10-1. *A Silva compass is set in stages.*

front of you with the direction-of-travel arrow pointing straight ahead. Continue to hold the compass in the same position, but turn your whole body until the red end of the needle points at N on the rim (FIG. 10-1D). Look up and you will be facing the direction you must go (FIG. 10-1E). Almost certainly you will see something you can use as a landmark, such as a tree, bush, rock, or a difference in ground level. Run to it, then repeat the procedure until you get to your destination.

Maps and Scales

For your own early orienteering competitions with friends, you will probably use the largest-scale map you have, then add *controls* (check points) and other information to it. For the best results, make photocopies of the part of the map you will be using, then add the new information with colored pens. Each competitor needs his or her own map, but you can prepare a master map and let each person copy what he or she needs.

If you enter a competition organized by an orienteering club, you usually will find that the maps have been specially prepared and are at a larger scale than you will have for ordinary use. Since the whole course is far from straight and could be arranged to finish near the start, the actual area covered is not vast. A very large-scale map need not require a large sheet of paper. A scale of 1:15,000 which is about 4 inches to 1 mile, is often used so that a lot of detail can be included.

Contour lines at close intervals are valuable to competitors because they need to know where moderate rises and falls are, as well as the more obvious hills and valleys. Closer lines than usual might be drawn in brown on an orienteering map. A 5-meter elevation interval (about 16 feet) is common. Much depends on the terrain. If it is nearly flat, the elevation intervals might be less. If it is very hilly, they could be more. In any case, the height differences should be the same all over the map. Check the legend for your particular map.

Look for the north-south magnetic lines that you will use for course setting. If you are using a modified standard map with true north at the top, the lines will be angled to suit.

Map Symbols

Orienteers need more information than can be obtained from a standard map. Besides landmarks, they need to know if they will be able to run, walk, or scramble. They need to know about obstructions that they might have to go around, fight through, or wade. They need to interpret the information quickly because time is all-important.

Color is a useful to reading the map quickly. If the maker of a special map has unlimited color available for printing, he or she could produce a helpful map that is very different from a standard map of the area. If he or she can reproduce only in black and white, the mapmaker might color the master map by hand and leave competitors to copy the colors on their own maps. When full coloring is available, graduations of color from orange to green indicate likely progress: orange is open land, shaded orange is semi open, light green shows vegetation and a slow run, medium green means walking, and dark green indicates vegetation you will have to fight through.

Many standard symbols are used, but some special ones are shown in FIG. 10-2. You should find an explanation of symbols on the border of a map or displayed near the start of a competition.

Equipment

Besides a map and compass, an orienteer carries a list of control points, in sequence, with a brief description of where they are and an identification code. In a normal event no one will be posted at a control point.

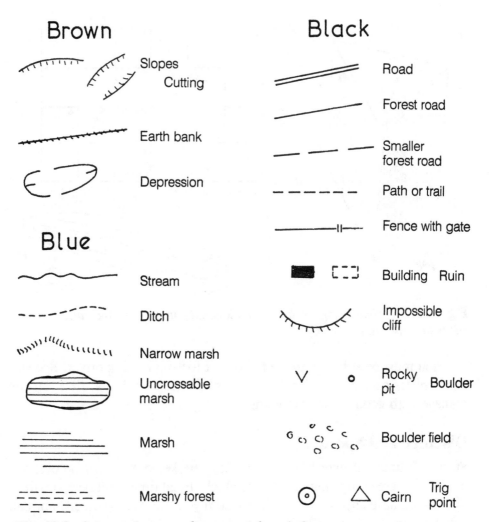

Fig. 10-2. *Orienteering maps have special symbols.*

Controls are marked with a folded fabric triangular assembly, with its faces divided diagonally into white and orange (FIG. 10-3A). The usual size is 30 cm (12 inches). Each competitor carries a control card (FIG. 10-3B). Details are written in the center. Spaces around the edge are numbered the same as the controls. At each control point, a pin punch (FIG. 10-3C), pierces a unique pattern. You punch in the correct space on the card to prove that you have been there.

An orienteer is expected to carry a whistle for use in emergency. He or she might also carry a map case with a transparent front, as well as cases for the control card and list.

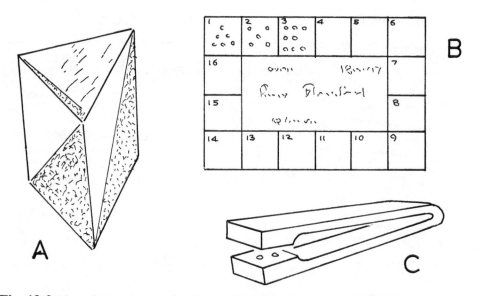

Fig. 10-3. *An orienteering marker has a diagonal pattern (A). You mark your card (B) with a special punch (C).*

You must be suitably dressed. Correct footwear is important. Specialist suppliers cater to the clothing needs of enthusiasts, but at first you can manage with good outdoor clothing.

Distance and Speed

Starts are timed at intervals. You might overtake someone or be overtaken, but you are competing against the clock. Final times will be compared. You do not have anyone else against whom you can pace yourself, nor can you copy anyone's direction.

You will spend much of your time estimating distances by counting paces, so you need to know your pace length at various speeds. It will not be the same walking as it is running. Mark out a distance of 100 meters as accurately as you can. Count your walking and running paces over this distance several times and work out averages. Make a note of the figures on something you always have with you when orienteering. The usual way to count paces is to count double steps—every time your right foot goes down, for instance.

You also might want to know how long it takes you to run or walk 100 meters. This estimate will help you judge distances by the time it takes you as well as by counting steps. It helps you to judge your progress in relation to the number of controls. You need to take many things into account. You might have to detour instead of going straight. Your pace will shorten and the time lengthen when you're going uphill. You might encounter obstructions to negotiate. You could waste time correcting mistakes.

Experience will teach you to judge distances and times in relation to what you see on the map and what you discover on the ground. When you have taken part in a few orienteering exercises, you will wonder what went wrong so often in earlier competitions.

Events

The size and length of an event is controlled by the area of land available. It could depend on the lay of the land; if it is difficult, controls might be fewer and closer together than if it is laid out in a more complex arrangement on easy ground. More than one course might be planned, with a shorter, easier route for beginners or those who want a more leisurely competition. The route must be challenging to make the event interesting. A beginners' event could be held in a park, but the experienced enthusiast expects rough country with natural woodland, vegetation, and other hazards.

At most events, start and finish are placed close together to provide convenient access and clothing storage, as well as to simplify organization. You register and are given a starting time, a control card, and any special instructions. A master map is posted so you can check your own map and mark it with the information you need.

The event will be arranged to take advantage of natural features, so routes between controls will vary in directions, but if the finish is near the start, the form will be roughly enclosed (FIG. 10-4A). An easy course might be arranged separately or by cutting out some of the controls (FIG. 10-4B). The distinctly marked controls will not be hidden, but because of natural features you might not see them until you are close. You are dependent on your compasswork and map-reading most of the time.

Keep an overall picture of the course in your mind, but concentrate on one control at a time. Convert the distance to paces, allowing for places where you will run or walk. Read the bearing from your map, then consider the hazards, possible diversions, and anything else that could stop you from following a direct route. Study contours. Moderate rises and falls will not matter, but look for signs of any cliffs or very steep slopes that you might have to go around. Remember that differences between heights of contour lines on an orienteering map are less than on most other maps, so do not get exaggerated ideas about slopes. Wider spaces between contour lines mean more modest slopes than where they are close (FIGS. 10-5A and B).

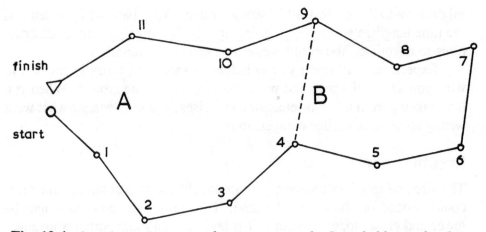

Fig. 10-4. *An orienteering course has many controls. It probably can be shortened for beginners.*

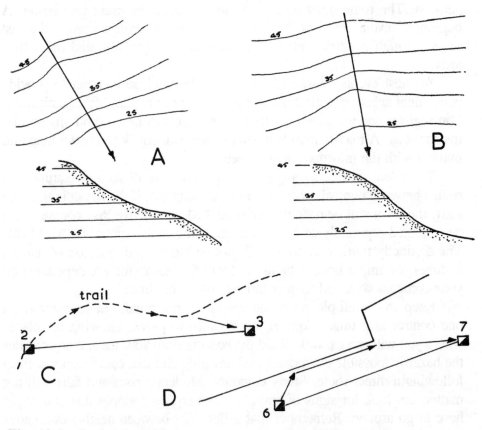

Fig. 10-5. *Contours indicate the type of slope(A and B). You must select from alternative routes (C and D) in an orienteering competition.*

You probably will not be competing in untouched forest or other land. The course might include man-made trails and roads, fences and walls, or possibly some buildings. In map-reading, these features are positive landmarks. They might also guide you in choosing a route. You might be wise to follow a trail part of the way, rather than try to go straight through the trees (FIG. 10-5C), where you might lose direction slightly.

Orienteers use the term *handrail* for a feature used as a guide. A hill or wall following your general direction can be noted as an indicator for at least part of the way (FIG. 10-5D).

You probably will have to work your way around an impossible hill or other obstruction and can use one of the methods of navigating described in chapter 8. If you have to reach a gate in a fence or some other spot on a line crossing your route, you should follow an offset course, so you know which way to turn when you get there.

Some of the skill in setting an orienteering competition and in interpreting it as a competitor is in arranging more than one possible route between controls. You must decide between routes. Do you go by a short route that involves scrambling or fighting your way through high vegetation? Do you take a longer route where you can walk or run on fairly flat ground? You have to balance your own skill and experience against the two routes. A third choice might take part of each route. The organizers do not tell you how to get between controls. You must decide the way.

The route to get from the last control to the finish line is usually clearly marked. You do not have to use a bearing for that. Overall time is what counts, so practice reading a direction from the map quickly and accurately. Punch your card and be ready to go as quickly as possible at a control. Memorizing map features and recognizing them on the ground will help. Avoid panic. If you cannot find a control, think logically about what might have gone wrong on the way from the last known point. Look the other way along the compass base for a reciprocal bearing. If necessary, go back to the last control and try again.

Nearly all orienteering events follow the pattern described, but other competitions can add variety. Some might provide interest among a group of friends on a local piece of ground or a town park.

In a *score event*, a large number of controls are given values according to their distance from the start. You have to visit as many controls as you can in a set time to try to collect the largest number of points. You choose the order in which you visit the controls and arrange the collection of points so that you get to the finish on time.

A relay event can be complicated if it has many competitors, but it can be exciting. Competitors start in one mass, then the first one in a team returns and touches off the second, and again with a third runner. To avoid crowding, some teams can tackle controls in a different order, but that adds to the complication.

Beginners can get useful experience by following a straight-line event. Markers are arranged out of sight of each other on a straight route. Cards are punched in the usual way. Starts are staggered in time. Each competitor must keep on the one bearing all the way and try to complete the course in the shortest time.

Night orienteering is not for beginners, but a shorter course with fewer problems might interest those with a little experience. Headlamps or flashlights are used to provide light.

In a map memory event, someone at each control point has a map of the route to the next marker. You look at that map and memorize the details, but you cannot take a map with you. This event is good training for regular orienteering because you learn to stop for map reading less often.

Although most orienteering is done by people on foot, you could arrange a similar event for horseback riders. If your area gets a lot of snow, you could follow the Scandinavian lead and arrange an orienteering event for skiers.

11

Sketching a Map

SOMEONE ASKS YOU HOW TO GET TO YOUR HOME. WHILE GIVING THE directions, you doodle a few lines on a piece of paper: "Go down 7th Avenue, over three crossings, then turn left at Lewis Road. About 200 feet along there, you will see the house on the right." Without thinking much about it, you have drawn a map (FIG. 11-1A). That crude sketch probably does more than your words to show the way.

Suppose you need to tell several people how to get to your home. They have never been in the area before and you have to mail directions to them. You could describe the way in words only, but they will find the house more easily if you include a sketch map, with or without a written description of the route. That map should be drawn more accurately than the first doodling, although it must give much the same information. This time you need to start with the way your visitors will approach. You must provide street names, and you should try to draw the map to an approximate scale. Make sure the reader knows which way up the map is oriented, particularly if north is not at the top. A visitor is unlikely to have a compass, but most people will assume that north is at the top. Drawing the map another way might be more convenient for you. Make sure the north arrow is prominent and that a line indicates scale distance (FIG. 11-1B).

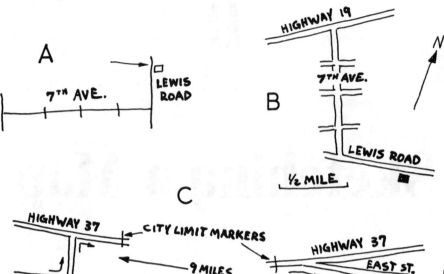

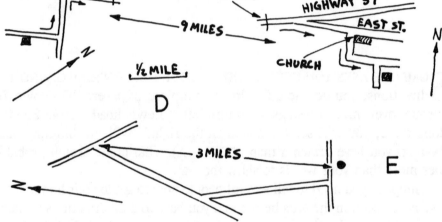

Fig. 11-1. *A sketch map might be simple and still tell all you need.*

Freehand Maps

Although the map is drawn freehand, try to keep it in reasonable proportion, with distances as accurate as possible and roads or other features in correct relation to each other. Draw roads as close parallel lines. You might include arrows to show the route. If you have to write down names or other information, write them some distance away and use arrows, rather than try to squeeze your writing into small spaces. A reasonably large sketch map is easier to read than a small one.

If you have to draw a sketch map covering a long distance, but most of the way is on one highway and you must provide detailed information at the ends, don't map the whole distance. You would end up with rather small detail where it is most needed at the ends. Instead, draw sketch maps at each end and indicate the distance between them along the highway, where your map reader runs no risk of getting lost (FIG. 11-1C).

Make sure you show all of the necessary information at both ends and make the beginning and end of the distance in between clear. Scales at the ends should be the same, but if the road between winds, you might want to show different compass bearings at the ends. A person using your map probably won't bother with a compass, since the directions you show should be enough but showing north erases all doubt. If you want to consider yourself a cartographer, include a scale and an indication of north on every map you draw, no matter how crude.

A scale might be a line indicating a distance (FIG. 11-1D), but the reader of your map will be concerned mainly with the distance between two points. He or she does not want the bother of scaling on a freehand map that might not be very accurate. In that case, you can just show a distance between key marks (FIG. 11-1E).

Sometimes sketch maps are needed for other purposes. Suppose your club is considering constructing a building in a recreation field (FIG. 11-2A). A sketch map can show the building in relation to the ground and any nearby buildings. You can pace the border of the field and the intended building space so you get the proportions right. That sketch will show where the new building must stand (FIG. 11-2B) so that the idea can be considered. A more accurate and measured map will be needed later.

You might need to show people where the place is in relation to other streets (FIG. 11-2C). You can use two approximate scales (FIG. 11-2D).

Measuring Distance

One problem you might have in making sketch maps is getting sizes and proportions accurate. You can use grid paper like that used for graphs and scientific drawings, but you should be able to show what you want on plain paper.

Many moderate distances can be measured by pacing. Learn the length of your average walking pace. If you know how many paces are needed for a set figure, say 100 yards, then you can estimate other distances in proportion. A simple way of counting is to use the orienteer's method of counting alternate steps—every time you put your right foot down, count 2, 4, 6, 8 and so on.

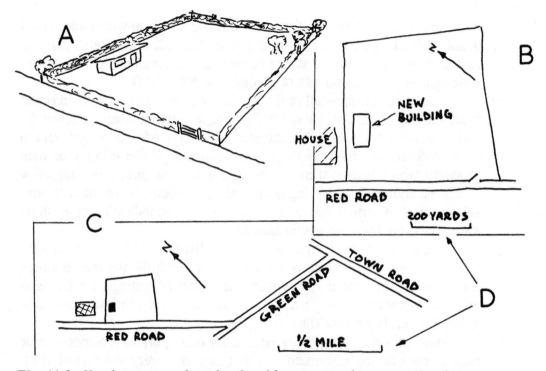

Fig. 11-2. *Sketch maps can show detail and location in relation to other places.*

You can adapt some artists' methods of estimating. An artist holds a pencil at arm's length to compare distant spacings. Suppose you look at a far fence and you know the distance between two posts. Stretch your arm and hold a pencil so the space between its end and your thumbnail cover that length when you sight with one eye (FIG. 11-3A). See how many of these sighted lengths go into the whole fence to find its total length.

You could pace your standard 100 yards along the fence and mark this distance with posts. If you go back and use the pencil sighting method to add up the number of sights you need in a long fence, the result might be more accurate than if you paced the whole way.

If you need to know the height of a building, you cannot pace it, but you can, in effect, turn it on its side and pace that. Have an assistant with a pole ready to move squarely to your line of sight. Stand at a good distance from the building holding a pencil vertically at arm's length. Adjust the amount of pencil projecting up so that its end is level with the top of the building and your thumbnail is at the bottom of the building as you sight with one eye (FIG. 11-3B). Without moving your body, turn your hand so that your thumbnail is still at the bottom of the building and the pencil end

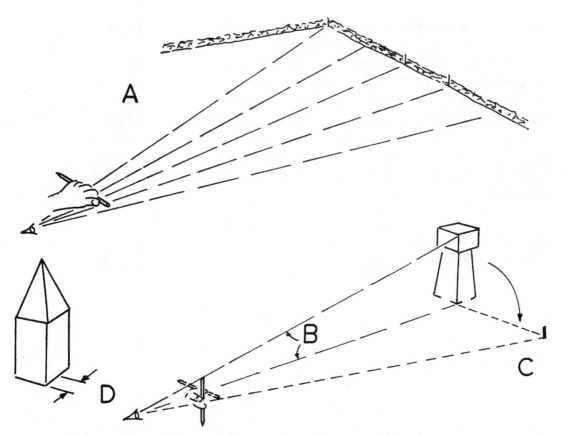

Fig. 11-3. *Sighting with a pencil aids in estimating distances and heights.*

projects to one side. Have your assistant move until you sight the pole through the pencil end (FIG. 11-3C). Pace the distance from the base of the building to the pole and you have a close approximation of the height of the building.

The top of the building you are measuring should be directly above the base position. If it is not, you will have to estimate how much distance to allow for the extra width at the base. For instance, a spire might be above a square base. You must add what you estimate or measure to be the distance from the center of the spire to the edge of the wall where you start pacing (FIG. 11-3D).

Another way to measure height is by proportion. Pace off 11 units from the object to be measured. The length of the units depends on the height of the object you are measuring. Longer distances give more accurate results. You need to go out farther than you guess the height to be. For example, a unit might be 5 paces, so you count off 55 paces. Put a pole vertically in the ground there or ask someone to hold it upright. Measure one more unit (5 paces) and mark that position (FIG. 11-4A).

At that position, lie flat on the ground so that your eye is as near the surface as you can get. Sight the top of the object across the pole. Have an assistant put a finger across the pole at your sight line (FIG. 11-4B). Measure the height of this mark in inches above the ground. The number of inches on the pole will be the same as the number of feet in height of the object you are measuring. As with the other method of measuring height, you must make allowances if the top is not directly over the spot where you start measuring.

Fig. 11-4. *You can measure a height by using a system of proportional triangles.*

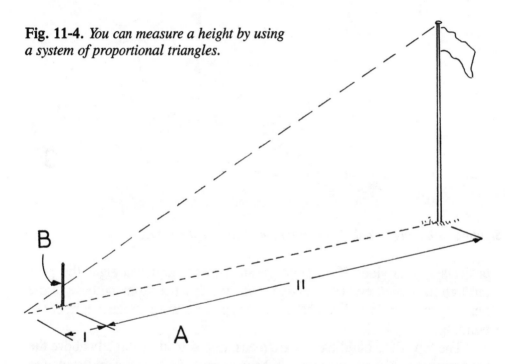

River Widths

Another interesting activity is determining a distance that cannot be paced, like a river width or the distance across a canyon or gully, without using elaborate equipment. A geometric method uses two similar triangles to find a line that can be paced or measured.

For example, suppose you want to measure across a river, probably 50 feet wide and running fairly straight where you want to measure it. Find a landmark, such as a tree, on the opposite bank, and select a point on the near side squarely opposite it (FIG. 11-5A). Mark this position with a stone

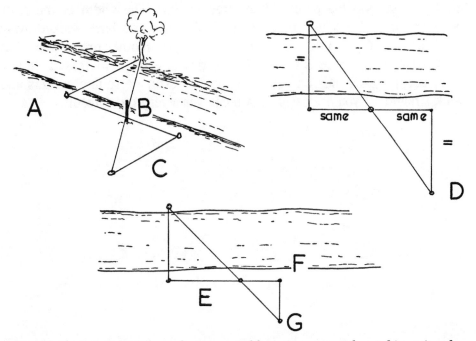

Fig. 11-5. *A river width can be measured by using reversed matching triangles.*

or pole. Walk squarely along the bank in a straight line any number of paces and plant a pole there (FIG. 11-5B). Continue on the same line the same number of paces and mark that position. The number of paces is not important as long as both sections are the same. If the total distance seems to be about the same as the width of the river, or more than that, the triangles will be in a proportion that should give a fairly accurate result.

From that point, walk away from the river at a right angle (FIG. 11-5C) until you reach a position where you can see the marker pole and the tree on the opposite bank in a straight line. The distance you have walked will be the same as the width across the river between the landmark on the far side and the first marker (FIG. 11-5D). You will have to subtract a little from the total width to allow for the distances of these two markers from the banks to get the actual width of the water.

You might have a problem if the amount of land you have available to use beside the river does not allow you to walk very far in a straight line from the first marker. You can use an arrangement of different-sized triangles. Suppose you walk 20 paces along the bank to place your sighting pole (FIG. 11-5E). Now walk 10 more paces to the place where you start walking away from the river (FIG. 11-5F). Walk away from the river at a right angle until you can see the pole and the tree in line. The width of the river between the markers will be double the distance you have walked away from the river (FIG. 11-5G). You can use triangles in other proportions, but if the triangle you pace is too small, the risk of error is increased. In any case, accuracy depends on you being able to estimate square corners and walk straight. If you are careful, you can get a very close result.

12

Making a Map

A SKETCH MAP CAN BE DRAWN QUICKLY AND WILL SERVE MANY purposes, but it cannot be as good as a map drawn to scale with all the features properly marked. For most of your needs, you can obtain maps that have been prepared by experts and tell you nearly all you want to know. Nearly all, but other information you need or are expected to provide might be missing.

You might be able to add the information to an existing map. You can get versions of some maps in faint outline form only, without color, so that you can use one as a base for a map to suit your own requirements. You might want to show the route for a car rally, a long-distance run, or a cycle ride.

One way of preparing additional information, instead of drawing on the actual map, is to put tracing paper over the map and draw in the extra details, followed by the roads and other key points that are important to the event. If you make photocopies of your tracing, you can give these special maps to all who need them. If you are adding this information for your own use, you can use the tracing and map together. With good tracing paper and clear lines on the map you are working over, you might be able to mark just the tracing with the new information, then put both in the photocopier so that the basic map markings show through as a faint background to your tracing paper markings.

You need to make a new map when you want to show features that are not on any standard map. Perhaps houses and roads have been built since the last map was made, or you want details on a much larger scale than is shown on any of the usual maps. You might want a fairly large-scale map of the details of a farm, its buildings, and field fences. Or you might need a map of a path or trail through woods, within an area perhaps less than 1/2 mile across.

Although you might not think that you could make a map, you can, using your compass and some simple equipment you can make. In map-making, you have to find directions and distances, then link them to make a map. Directions will be in degrees, obtained from the compass, or by other means of sighting described later in the chapter. Distances can be measured by pacing, by using the odometer in the car, or by using some other sort of measure, such as a rope of a known length.

You need paper and something to which it can be taped to keep it flat, such as a piece of plywood. You also need a rule to measure and draw straight lines. You can use your compass as a protractor, but marking angles on the map will be easier with a separate protractor. One that covers a full circle is better than the more usual semicircular type, but either kind will work.

For some mapping, you can make an actual map as you survey the land. In other places, you should make notes of bearings and distances in the field, and make a map from this information later. In both methods, you will put lines on the first map that might not be part of the final map, so be prepared to work in two stages. When you have all the information mapped, you might be able to erase unwanted lines, although you might do better to trace what is wanted onto the final map, with symbols and other information added, and then add a scale, a north arrow, and a border, so you can make prints of an attractive map.

Line Survey

Suppose you want to make a map of a path that goes from the edge of a property to a pond and divides there into two paths that lead to exit gates. This kind of map is called a *line survey*. Make a sketch map (FIG. 12-1A) so that you have a general idea of the layout. Don't worry if the sketch is rough and inaccurate, since you will throw it away later.

Divide the path into reasonably straight sections. Have a helper hold a pole upright at the end of the first straight section. Sight the pole from the starting point with your compass and note the bearing (FIG. 12-1B). Measure the distance to the pole. Make notes of the bearing and distance (FIG. 12-1C).

Move to the first pole position with your compass while your assistant takes the pole to the end of the next straight section (FIG. 12-1D). Sight and measure again. You can put your results alongside the parts of your sketch map or make a separate list. Continue on to where the paths divide. Follow one path with distances and bearings, then go back and do the same on the other path. Be careful not to confuse readings. You can letter them on your sketch map and list to help you keep track.

Measure the pond as accurately as you can. You should be able to draw it on the final map so that it is fairly accurate in shape and size. Measure the widths of the paths at various places. You might find one branch is wider than the other, or it might widen at the pond. If the final map is to large a scale, you can show actual widths of paths. If the scale is smaller or the widths do not matter, you can draw the paths all the same width.

You have completed the work that must be done outdoors. You can draw the first scale map anywhere. You now know the overall size of the paths to be mapped and must decide on a scale that will put the map on paper of a suitable size. If you want to make copies on a photocopier, you will have to use paper that is within its limits. Your scale is likely to be in feet, rather than miles. Decide how much 1 inch will represent. Remember, you want to measure on the map with an ordinary rule, so pick something that allows easy divisions of an inch, such as 400 or 800 feet long to 1 inch. Then you can use the fraction markings on the rule.

If you start with a large piece of paper, you do not have to worry if the map develops at an unexpected angle to the paper shape. You can trace the final outline at a different angle onto another sheet of paper, providing you show north on it.

Draw a north-south line where you intend to start the mapped path. Put a mark on it for the starting point, then draw a line, or *traverse*, at the first angle you surveyed (FIG. 12-1E). Measure the first scale distance along it. Put another north-south line there and draw the next bearing line (FIG. 12-1F). At that point, mark the next bearing line and its length, and so on to the end, including the forking path.

Now you have a map of the center lines of the paths. If you will be drawing to scale widths, mark the key widths at several places and draw the path outlines. If not, draw parallel lines for the outlines of the paths, but keep the drawn widths narrow for neatness. Round corners and allow for any waviness you have noticed between points (FIG. 12-1G). Draw the pond

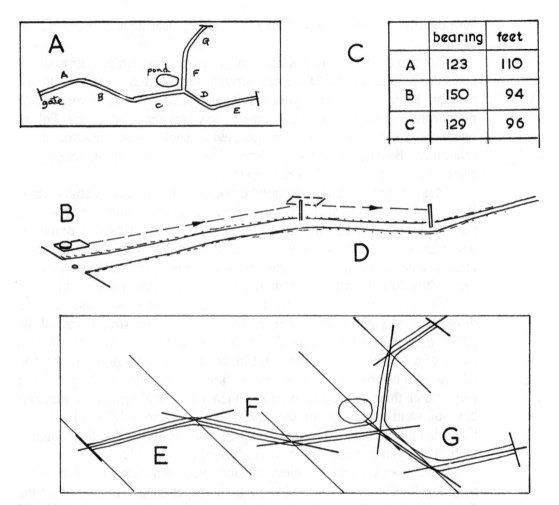

	bearing	feet
A	123	110
B	150	94
C	129	96

Fig. 12-1. *Begin a compass survey of a path with a sketch map, then sight and measure sections.*

as close to scale as you can. You might want to show other features, such as a bench, a sign, or a special tree. Measure along the path to get their correct locations. You cannot measure and show contours, but if one part of the path is obviously higher than another, you can mark it with an arrow showing the direction of the slope.

Now your map has all the necessary information, as well as some unnecessary lines that can be erased. If you want to produce a map that looks good, trace the lines that matter and add a scale, a north point, and a title, all within a border. You also can add your name and the date (FIG. 12-2).

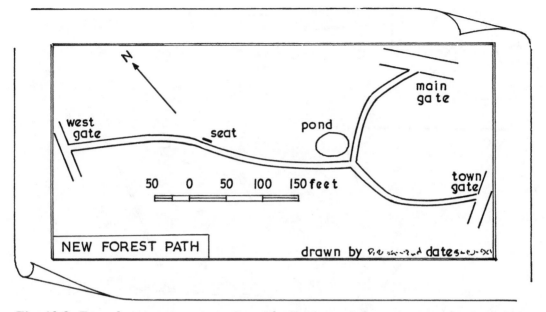

Fig. 12-2. *From the survey, you can extract the important information to make the finished map.*

Triangulation

Triangles are among the most important shapes in mapmaking and surveying. The great thing about a triangle is that you cannot push it out of shape. Once you have the three sides, the three angles, or any combination of them, the triangle can be one shape.

If you look at a three-sided figure (FIG. 12-3A), it has a shape that cannot be altered. If a figure has four or more sides, the combination of sides and angles can be moved about to make a variety of shapes (FIG. 12-3B).

If you take a baseline of a known length and draw lines at any chosen angles from its ends, only one triangle can be produced by that combination of one side and two angles (FIG. 12-3C). You can use this fact to locate a point in relation to two others. I already discussed this method in earlier examples of taking cross bearings. In mapmaking, it is called *triangulation*.

Suppose you are traveling along a road and you take a bearing of a house (FIG. 12-3D). Then you measure the distance you go along the road to another point and take a bearing there (FIG. 12-3E). Drawn on a map, the sight lines will cross at the position of the house.

You do not need to measure the distance along the road if you can identify places on the ground and on an existing map. You can take bearings

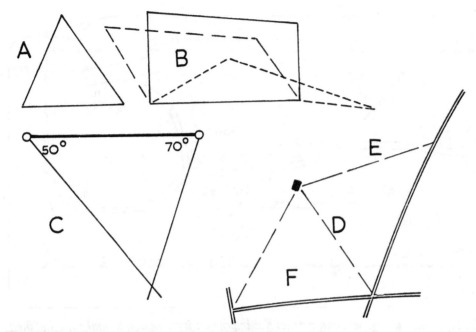

Fig. 12-3. *A figure with three sides holds its shape. A figure with a greater number of sides might become distorted. Surveying uses triangles.*

from them (FIG. 12-3F) knowing that the actual distance and the scale distance will match. Triangulation is the basis of much mapmaking, even when elaborate instruments are used.

Sometimes you have to build triangles on triangles. If many places are visible from the two ends of your baseline, you can take bearings on all of them and the sight lines will make a rather complex pattern, but you will have spotted all the places (FIG. 12-4A). One or more places you want to locate might be hidden by trees or hills from one end of your baseline. You can take the position where the point is in view and one of the other places you have located as the ends of a new baseline (FIG. 12-4B). Sight from these points, and you have another triangle and the new position to plot on your map (FIG. 12-4C).

The most accurate plotted positions come when sight lines cross almost at right angles (FIG. 12-4D). You can still get an accurate plot if the lines are a long way out of square, but accuracy is easier if you avoid very *obtuse* (greater than 90°) crossings (FIG. 12-4E) or very *acute* (less than 90°) angles of crossing (FIG. 12-4F). In extreme cases, the thickness of a pencil line can make a considerable difference to a position on a small-scale map.

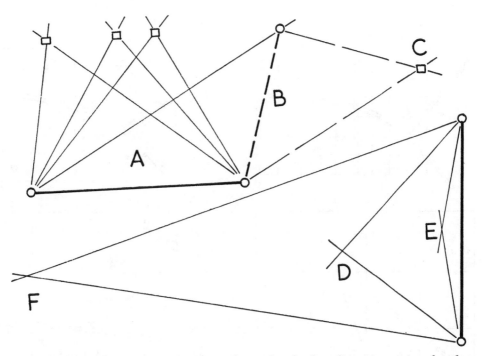

Fig. 12-4. *Making many sights from the ends of a baseline gives triangles that provide accurate positions.*

Road Survey

As you have seen, if you need more details than an existing map shows, you can survey the new features and add them to the map or to a tracing of it. A problem arises when the existing map has too small a scale and you have no space to make the additions you want. Your best plan then is to enlarge the part you need and make the additions to that. This way you will have a local map large enough for the details to be easily seen.

Some photocopiers will enlarge illustrations, but only to a limit, probably twice the original size. That size might be enough for your needs. If you want a bigger map of a smaller area, you will have to draw a new map.

You can get a fairly accurate result by using grids of squares. Suppose you want the new map to be three times as large as the original part. Draw a pattern of squares on the part of the original map you wish to enlarge (FIG. 12-5A). Draw another pattern of the same number of squares on the plain paper, making these squares three times as large as those on the original map (FIG. 12-5B). The number of squares in an area depends on how much detail you want to copy and the degree of accuracy needed. You could

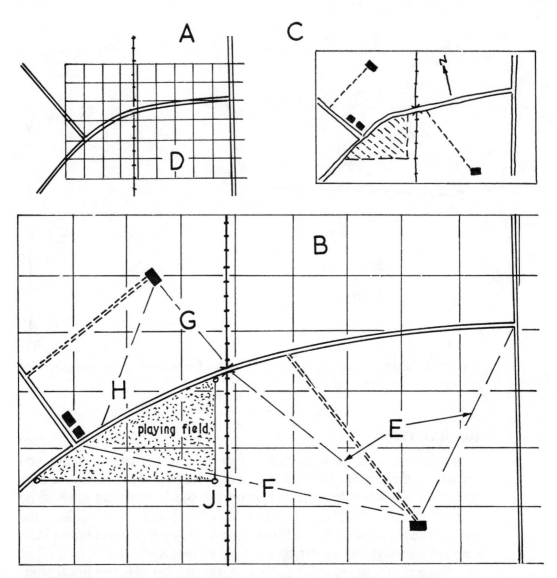

Fig. 12-5. *You can enlarge details on a map using squares. Make additions by using triangular sightings.*

have 1/4-inch or 1/2-inch squares on the original map, then 3/4-inch or 1 1/2-inch squares for the enlarged copy.

Preparing a freehand sketch map of the area you want to cover can be helpful (FIG. 12-5C). In the example, the original small-scale map shows only highways and a railroad (FIG. 12-5D). In your sketch map, you show that you want to include several houses, two dirt roads, and a proposed playing field. Before you can get permission for the playing field, you must produce a detailed map showing it and nearby houses.

One square at a time, draw from the original map the details you want in the appropriate larger square, noting the proportionate positions where map lines cross the grid lines. Straight lines are easy and can be filled in first. You will have to fill in other details freehand, but they should be fairly accurate if you watch line crossing positions. Once you have copied all the details you need, you can erase the grid squares on your enlarged map.

The positions of the two houses that lie away from the road are important. You can take bearings of the lower house from the railroad bridge and the eastern road junction (FIG. 12-5E). If that house is within view of the other road junction, you can take a bearing from there as well (FIG. 12-5F). That bearing covers a longer distance and a more acute angle, but if its plotted line comes fairly close to the crossing of the other two, it will confirm the position. You can measure down the road that runs south to a point nearly opposite the house and take another bearing from there, if you want another check. If all the sights do not cross on one spot when you plot them, you will have to judge which seem to be most accurate. Measure the distance from the railroad bridge to the end of the dirt road and draw it to scale on your map.

You should be able to get a good bearing on the other isolated house from the railroad bridge (FIG. 12-5G), but if a view from the western road junction is obscured by a house, you will have to measure along the road to a point where you can see it (FIG. 12-5H). Site from there and mark this position to scale on your map. Measure to the end of the dirt road and draw it.

The positions and sizes of the roadside houses can be found by measuring. Draw them on your map.

Mark the position of the proposed playing field with corner posts where it will touch the road and at the southern corner where it will come near the railroad track (FIG. 12-5J). You might be able to draw the boundaries by measuring, but take bearings of the corner pole from the bridge and the western road junction to verify the results you get by measuring.

From these results, you will have enough information for your final map, which should be drawn neatly within a border, and with a scale and north point, similar to the path map. You can adapt these methods to your own needs and area. Use triangulation. Take two bearings on each feature and try to arrange a third bearing to confirm the position. If you have to draw new roads or trails, take bearings, even if sometimes they appear to be square to an existing road. Angles can be deceptive.

Area Survey

One interesting way to make a map is to do an *area survey*. In an area survey, you stand near the middle of the property so that you can see all around. This property might be a field or town park. You can practice on a small scale by surveying your own yard. The method is the same, whatever the size of the area. Arrange a baseline anywhere in the area so that you can see all corners and other features from both ends of it. The length of the baseline is not important, but between one-fourth and one-third of the distance across the space usually is suitable. The line will be used as a base for triangulating and should be measured carefully (FIG. 12-6A). Draw it to scale on the paper that will take the map (FIG. 12-6B). You will have to estimate the overall size of the land and choose a scale that will fit the map on the paper. You do not have to draw the line on the ground, but you should set markers at each end of it. Short posts pushed into the ground are suitable.

As with the earlier examples, making a freehand sketch map first is helpful (FIG. 12-6C). This sketch will show you the general shape and the best place to arrange the baseline. Let the ends of the line point towards long straight parts of the outline, to reduce the number of acute, and possibly inaccurate, angles in the triangles.

You need to take bearings of all features, such as corners, gates, trees, and anything else you want to include, from both ends of the baseline. As you get the bearings with your compass, record them in lists on a clipboard or in a notebook (FIG. 12-6D) so that you can transfer the details to your map. Take the bearings in turn from each end of the baseline in a clockwise direction. You could number the bearings from one end of the line and letter those from the other end.

Start by establishing the bearing of the baseline. Stand over one marker and sight the other. Note the result.

Stand over a marker and sight with your compass to take and record bearings of every corner and any other feature you want to put on the map (FIG. 12-6E). Move to the other marker and do the same (FIG. 12-6F). If you plan to include isolated items, such as trees, you might prefer to keep their bearings recorded separately.

Make sure the paper for the map or plan is big enough. You can trim it to a smaller size after the map has been drawn. Note the bearing of the baseline and, using that, draw north-south lines through the ends of the map baseline, so that you can orient your protractor readings to them (FIG. 12-6G).

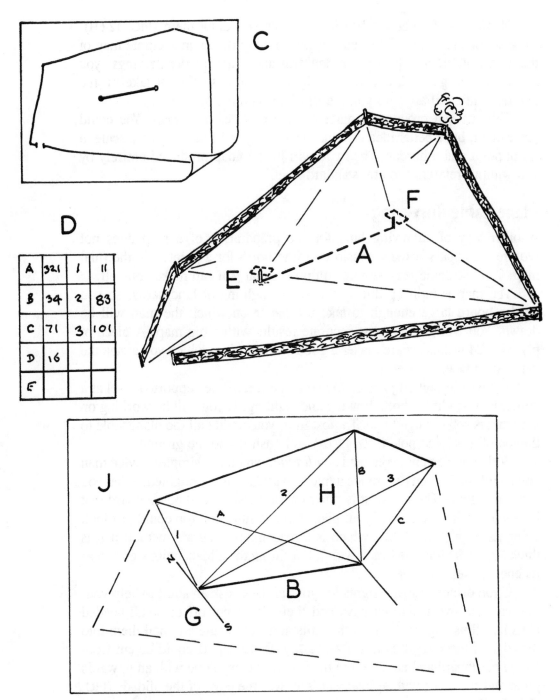

Fig. 12-6. *You can survey a field from the ends of a central baseline on the ground and on the paper that will be the map.*

Number and letter the bearing lines as you draw them (FIG. 12-6H). Linking the crossings of the sight lines should build up an accurate map of the area (FIG. 12-6J). If you are doubtful about any of the bearings, you might have to go back and do the sighting again, so do not take up the markers until you are sure you are finished with them.

This method produces a maze of bearing lines on a map. You could erase them, but a better idea is to make a tracing and finish it with a scale, a north point and a border. Then you will have a map produced entirely by you without reference to any standard map.

Plane Table Surveying

Another way of surveying land for the preparation of a map does not require a compass, except possibly to find north for a pointer on the final map. You use some very simple equipment that you can make yourself.

The map is built up during the actual sighting of landmarks, so you need a board large enough to take the paper on which the map will be drawn. You will get the most accurate results with a big map. A piece of plywood 24 inches square makes a good *plane table* to which you attach the paper with tape.

You will be sighting across the table, so it must be supported level at a convenient height for both drawing and sighting. If you will be working on land that is soft enough to push a post into, you could nail the plane table to the top of a pointed pole (FIG. 12-7A) and push it into the ground.

With a plane table, you need an *alidade*, which is a simpler device than you might think from its strange name. An alidade is a straightedge that you can sight along. The longer it is, the more accurate it will be—a board that is as long as the diagonal of your plane table is suitable. You could just look along its edge (FIG. 12-7B), which is a reasonably accurate method if it is thick ($1/2$ inch high and 1 inch wide), but fitting the alidade with sights near its ends makes it easier to use.

If you decide to make sights for your alidade, ask an adult to help you. You can use two nails that have had their heads cut off or small-headed nails like finishing nails. Bend the nails at a right angle and nail them into the edge of the straight board (FIG. 12-7C). Better sights could be cut from sturdy cardboard and nailed on to the board. Arrange one with an upwards point and the other with a downwards V over the edge of the alidade (FIG. 12-7D).

You need a ruler for measuring on the map and some means of measuring on the ground. You can rely on pacing or use a piece of rope of a known

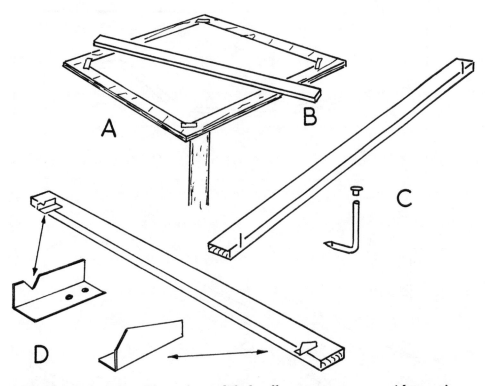

Fig. 12-7. *A plane table and an alidade allow you to survey without using a compass.*

length. Use a soft pencil so that you can erase lines if you make a mistake. Now you are ready to start.

A suitable example for practice might be a trail that runs among a few isolated trees. A freehand sketch map will help you see what has to be done to make a map of the trail and trees (FIG. 12-8A). First map the trail, then get the positions of the trees in relation to it. Estimate the length and width of the area concerned, then choose a scale that will allow it all to fit on the paper.

Set up your plane table at one end of the trail. Send a helper with a pole as far along the trail as you can see in a straight line. Measure this distance. Sight across the plane table in a suitable position that allows you to draw in the rest of the map. Draw along the edge of the alidade and mark a scale distance along this line (FIG. 12-8C).

Go to the position of the sighting pole and send your helper to another point along the trail. Set up the plane table and sight back along the line of the trail on the map to your start to orient the map to the land (FIG. 12-8D).

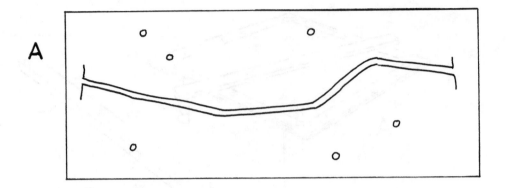

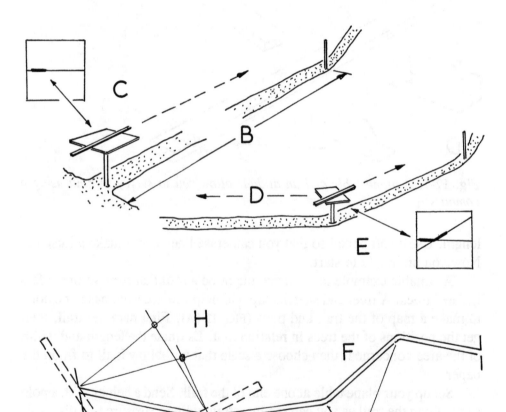

Fig. 12-8. *A path and the location of some trees can be surveyed directly with a plane table and alidade.*

Now sight the next pole position through the mark you have made to indicate the end of the first section. Measure and mark this part of the trail (FIG. 12-8E). Continue in this way until you have mapped the whole trail.

You can outline the trail on your map with parallel lines (FIG. 12-8F) to avoid confusion with other lines you will be adding.

Finding the positions of the trees is done by taking cross bearings from different positions on the path. In most cases you can use the pole positions that you used for surveying the trail. Go to these spots with the plane table. Sight along the trail to orient it, then sight the trees along the alidade and draw sight lines of ample length (FIG. 12-8G). Go to other positions and do the same so that you have triangles that give you the positions of the trees (FIG. 12-8H). For some tree positions, you might sight from three places to provide a check on locations (FIG. 12-8J).

In this first plane table survey, I suggest you complete the trail first, then go back to add trees to the map. When you have become more familiar with plane table surveying, you can take all the sights from one spot at the same time, but be careful not to mistake one of the many lines for another. Mark each in some way so that you can tell them apart.

This method of surveying involves a large number of construction lines that are not needed in the final map. Trace the parts that you want, then complete the tracing as a final map with a border containing a scale, a north point, a title, and any other information that you want to include.

You can use a plane table and alidade instead of a compass for surveying and mapping an enclosed area such as that in FIG. 12-6. You need the same markings for the end of a line on the ground and a matching scale line on your map (FIG. 12-6A and B). Tape paper on the plane table. Set the table up at one end of the line on the ground and orient it by sighting the other marker with the alidade laid along the map line. Hold the alidade through the mapped end of the line you are standing over and sight every corner and every feature you want to locate. Go to the other marker on the ground, orient the map again, then sight all the same places. Join the points of the triangles drawn to get the outline of the area. When many sights are to be made with the alidade through one spot on the map, you can put a pin at the spot and pivot the alidade edge against it. You don't need to draw the full length of every sight line. The lines will be less confusing if you only draw the outer parts where you judge the other lines will cross. Put an identification mark on each line.

The resulting map should look the same as the one you made using a compass. You have drawn your map directly in the middle of the field, instead of noting a large number of compass bearings, transferring them with a protractor, and drawing the map elsewhere. Occasionally, one method will be preferable to the other, so you should know both of them. Sometimes you can use both methods. In the example of the trail and trees, you could use the plane table and alidade to survey the path, then find the positions of the trees with a compass, if bad weather forces you to work on the map indoors.

13

Mapping Afloat

WHEN YOU ARE FLOATING ON WATER, THE FEATURES AROUND YOU that affect mapping are the reverse of those ashore. On land, heights are measured above sea level. When you are afloat, the contours are below you; you are concerned with depths. A great many other features can be seen ashore. Many features might be below the water, but most of them cannot be seen. These differences mean that maps concerned with water must be prepared in a different way than maps of land. Even when the vessel is in sight of land, the features needed by a person navigating a boat are different from those needed by a person walking or driving near the shore.

How different the maps are depends on the body of water. If you are traveling down a river in a canoe or kayak, you are still very concerned with features on land. They indicate your location, your access to land, and your progress. If you are boating in a river estuary or small bay, you might still want to know about places ashore, but you also need guidance on sandbanks and rocks that might be exposed at low tide. You need to know how much water is under the boat in various places. You need to know about marks that have been put on the shore to help navigation. If you are cruising offshore, your mapping needs are completely different from your needs on land. Your map, which is called a *chart*, is nothing like a shore map.

If you are going boating, particularly if you are going away from the shore, learn all you can about seamanship. If things go wrong on land, they might create just a nuisance. If things go wrong on water, the problem could become serious or even fatal. Even boating in a tidal estuary can be hazardous. This book does not cover the handling of any sort of craft—get information and instruction elsewhere. Then you can go afloat with confidence.

Canoeing Rivers

A canoe or kayak will float in a few inches of water, so rivers inaccessible to other craft can be used. Some of these rivers include rapids or falls, which add to the interest of the expedition for the experienced canoeist or kayaker. Modern kayaks are capable of dealing with rapid rivers that would have been considered impassable a few years ago. But more than the kayak must be capable; you need to know how to handle the craft on white water. From a map or other source, you want to find out if the river is placid or rapid. Are you skilled enough to venture on this particular river?

General maps do not tell you much about rivers. On some maps intended for motorists, even finding the rivers can be difficult. Since a river flows from high to low ground, its headwaters must be higher than its lower reaches. You can assume that near its source it is not very big, but that it broadens and gathers more water as it progresses, particularly if it is joined by tributaries, which might be small streams or large rivers. If the map shows the source of the river, a canoe or kayak is unlikely to be able to float within a few miles of that. The points of interest on the river must be some distance downriver.

Look at contours that cross the river line. If they are fairly close, the river drops steeply. It might contain rapids or progress through a series of falls. Usually, the contours are wider apart farther down the river, showing that it will have a milder progress there. Downriver might have lesser rapids, an even, fast flow, or, if it has broadened, a moderate flow. If the river reaches a plain and contours are very far apart, the river almost certainly will be broad and slow. If contour lines dip back in an upstream direction, the water has worn the ground away, and the river will be below the level of surrounding land, if not in an actual gorge.

In this way, you have gathered quite a lot of information from a map that was not designed to provide waterway details. But if you want to take your canoe or kayak on the river, you will need to know more. If the river has been canoed frequently, someone might have produced a detailed map of it. An information center in a nearby town might know if such a map has been made. A local canoe or kayak club should be able to help you. River maps are usually arranged in a series of strips for convenience in handling and to allow for alterations in direction (FIG. 4-6). To show the necessary details they will be to a larger scale than local general maps.

Suppose you are unable to find a special river map, but decide to go ahead with the information that you obtained from a general map. Trace the river from the general map. Include bridges and any nearby land features that seem important. With most rivers, you will be surprised at how much the river twists, apart from any large changes of direction.

Even if you trace the river from the largest-scale map you can find, it might not be big enough to allow space for details of river features that you want to add. Using a photocopier or the squares method (chapter 12), enlarge the map so that the scale is at least 1 inch to 1 mile. Divide the enlarged map into pieces of manageable size. Make prints you can take with you. Mark river miles from the first launch place as closely as you can measure and estimate them. Take along your general map for reference to land details.

When you are on the river, add all the details you can. You might not use all of them on a final map, but you are better off having some information you discard than leaving gaps along the way. Use your compass and note directions from time to time. You might think the river always runs in one direction because you can see it in front of you, but in a mile you might have actually turned completely around in relation to north.

After the trip, you can assemble all the river information you have added and make a map of it. You have been an explorer, even if the land around the river has been mapped in detail. The river might be the only piece of the area previously unexplored in detail from the water user's point of view.

Your final map might be assembled in strips, all to the same scale, with north arrows noting changes in direction. You could include a title and some notes, as well as a key to any special symbols or markings you have used. If you want the map to be most useful, you will have to write down quite a lot of information, with arrows connecting it to the parts of the river concerned. If the river contains rapids, and you are familiar with the international grading of rivers, you can insert that information. Briefly, grade I water is almost placid, possibly with just a slight speeding up of the current in places; grade II might contain simple rapids that should not be a problem to anyone with a little experience; grade III begins to get more exciting, although still not much of a problem; grade IV and higher are dangerous unless you are very experienced.

Put the map together neatly. Allow a good overlap of sections. You will show your skill as a mapmaking explorer. The map should be of use to others who follow, so you might want to print and distribute copies (FIG. 13-1).

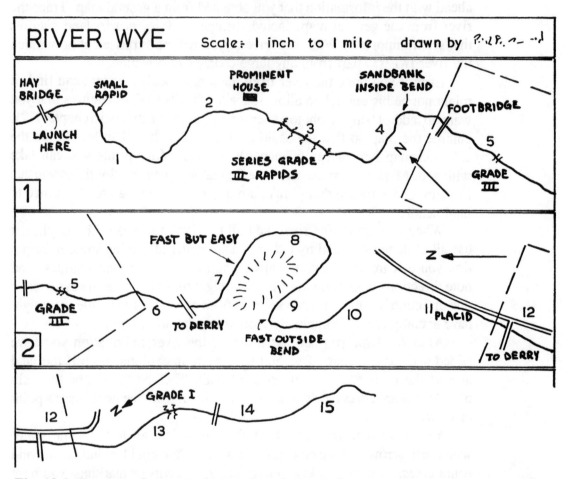

Fig. 13-1. *You can make a map of a river based on an enlargement from another map and then draw in your additional information.*

Navigable Rivers

If a river is navigable, or suitable for craft larger than canoes and kayaks, river maps will almost certainly be in existence. If it is a large river, like the Mississippi, the maps will be a series of very detailed large-scale charts giving all the information needed by navigators of large commercial craft traveling long distances. The river will have many navigation marks on the banks, *buoys* will mark shallows, and bridges will be marked for passage. The amount of guidance for craft of considerable *draft* will be marked on the sections of river maps.

Smaller rivers might not carry commercial craft, but pleasure boats probably travel them. Some of theses boats might sit quite low in the water, and their operators need to know where the channels are. Shore markers and buoys will be similar to those on larger rivers, but usually of more modest size. You should be able to find published maps for those rivers popular with pleasure boaters. Some of these maps will be prepared officially, but others might be prepared by boat rental firms or others interested in the river. The official maps are strictly factual. Some of the others might look more attractive, but be careful to check that the vital information is all there and correct. Pictorial treatment with a wide use of colors could be covering inaccuracies.

If rivers of any size are used at night, a range of lights indicates marks on the banks or buoys in the water. These lights should all be shown on the maps. On a clear day, most rivers are navigable by sight, but in poor visibility or after dark, using a compass to help you to interpret the map is advisable.

River maps are provided to help you navigate. Most of them do not show much about adjoining country. Towns, details of docks, and other access points might be indicated. The access roads on each side of bridges might not be drawn very far, and the river map might not even show you where those roads go. If all you want to do is travel along the river with a minimum of trouble, the river map tells you all you need, but if you want to go ashore, you will need general maps of the area as well. You might need road access. You might want to buy supplies. For these purposes, you need to look at a map of the surrounding country as well as the river map, which might tell you the best place to land, but not where to go once you have landed.

The symbols used on river maps are not all the same, but each map or chart should be accompanied by a key or legend so that you can identify the symbols. Some symbols might only have slight differences to indicate colors or other features of the buoy or other object. If the waterway is extensive and the chart sections are drawn to a fairly large scale, each sheet might be on stiff, water-resistant, spiral-bound paper so that charts can be changed quickly and opened flat.

A good example of a river map is the set of Ohio River navigation charts issued by the United States Army Corps of Engineers. Each page is about 8 inches by 14 inches and the charts are drawn to a scale of 1 inch to 2000 feet. This size is sufficient for the width of the river and positions on it to be shown without crowding. To guide deep-draft commercial traffic, a line shows the center of the deep channel and another line backed by black dots shows where the depth is less than 9 feet. Water is colored blue (FIG. 13-2A).

Buoys mark the limits of the navigable channel. A small circle shows the actual position, but a diamond shape draws attention to it. Opposite sides of the channel are marked by *can* (black) and *nun* (red) buoys, which are named for their shapes. A can buoy is cylindrical and a nun buoy is tapered. If the buoy will be lit at night, the small circle has a larger red one around it (FIG. 13-2B). A light on the bank is also shown as a red circle with a black center. A *daymark* (one that is not lit at night) is shown as a triangle (FIG. 13-2C).

Lights on the bank are not always lit continuously or in one color. Some are identified by flashing at measured intervals. The characteristic signal of each light is shown in abbreviated form near its symbol. For instance, "GpFl.W.5 sec.,2 flashes" means the light flashes in two groups of white light showing 2 flashes of 5 seconds each. Colors of lights could be white or red on the left bank when going downstream and white or green

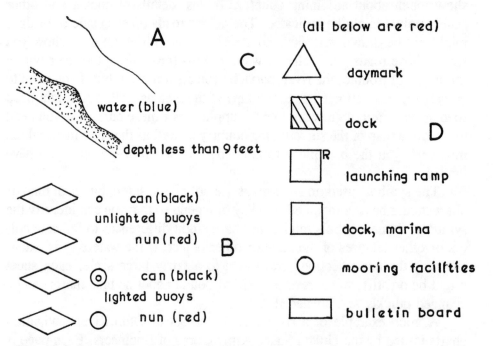

Fig. 13-2. *Maps of navigable rivers have their own symbols.*

on the right bank. Flashing arrangements will be different from all others in the vicinity, although they could be repeated on part of the river distant enough to prevent any confusion.

Many river symbols are self-explanatory (FIG. 13-2D) when you refer to the legend. Each chart has a scale that is most conveniently used with dividers. North is indicated. Map strips overlap for ease of continuous navigation, and the overlap of each pair is marked by a match line. As with canoeing maps, north will often be in a different position on adjoining sheets to allow for twists in the river. An arrow shows the direction of flow of the river, and numbered mile-post positions are marked on the chart (FIG. 13-3).

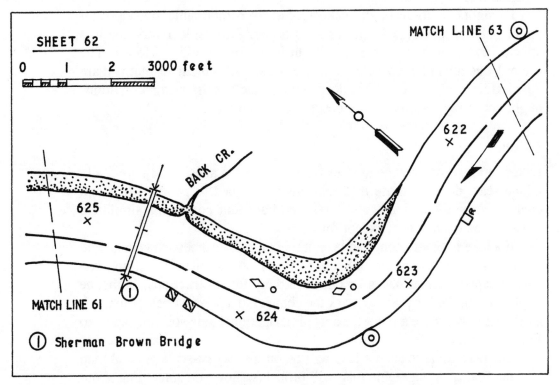

Fig. 13-3. *This map of part of a navigable rivers shows the use of symbols.*

Some additional information is given on the back of a chart. Pictures of bridges and clearance of aerial power lines are important to navigators of large craft. A large boat might have to be lined up carefully to suit the size of a bridge arch. If you are in a smaller craft, the pictures help you recognize and confirm where you are.

Water level can affect navigation on inland waters. Heavy rainfall can raise the level of a rapid river by several feet, possibly for only a few hours. This rise affects the character of a river considerably. The river might become fast all the way, so that all the marked rapids are covered. The extra water it might have removed the hazards of rocky rapids, but you might be swept into three branches. A swollen river of this type should be considered very dangerous for kayaks or canoes.

More water in a navigable river might increase the current to the stage where upstream progress is impossible, and downstream travel becomes difficult because of the problem of stopping. Locks might cease to be usable. Your map covers normal conditions—if they are exceptional, heed local advice.

Drought conditions might make a rapid river impossible to navigate; it might only be passable in places by wading. Navigable rivers are less affected by drought, but channels might be narrower and shallower. The use of locks might be restricted to conserve water. Remember that you are not dealing with land, which does not change much, water conditions might not always be as they are described on the map.

Lakes

Lakes and reservoirs range in sizes from the Great Lakes, which are really inland seas, down to those that are better described as ponds. Maps and charts for the Great Lakes must take into account conditions similar to those on the open ocean, except for tides.

If a lake is small enough to be suitable only for canoes, rowboats, and small sailing craft, you are unlikely to find a special map for it, and you cannot expect to find buoys or other markers for obstructions. Someone might have pushed in posts to mark the channel to a private dock or to mark a mudbank, but these are not the sort of navigational aids you can expect to find on a map.

The best guide to such a lake will be on the largest-scale general map you can find. A topographic map will probably show you something about the land bordering the lake. It will show marshes. It will show which parts are wooded and which are open. It might show underwater contours or soundings. If you will be using a canoe, depths do not matter much, but if you want to use a sailboat that draw 36 inches with its keel, soundings are important. Even with a canoe or kayak, you would be glad to know where you can expect enough depth to allow you to launch close to the shore. Underwater contour lines closer to the shore there than elsewhere will alert you to such a place. If the lines are widely spread, the bottom shelves at only a slight angle and you might have to wade some ways offshore.

If the lake is larger and used by fishing and other craft, a map prepared by a fishing or boating club or a boat rental firm might be available. You might find that shallows have been marked with buoys or driven posts and indicated on the map. The posts might have top marks to make them more obvious. If the lake has an island, a shallow extending from it might be marked. The accessway to a launching ramp or dock probably will have its deep channel marked. These things might be shown on a locally prepared map with unusual symbols. If no map is available, and you intend to use the lake frequently, you could prepare a navigational map of the lake based on the best map you can find with extra information added.

Many lakes are connected to rivers. A river might flow in at one side. It, or another river, might flow out at another side. If it is a navigable river, you can expect to find buoys and other markings on the lake to match those on the river. A channel across the lake will be marked by two rows of buoys. Buoyed channels to docks or other landing places might also be marked. In this case, details of the lake will be on the river map.

If smaller rivers are connected to the lakes, few or no navigational aids might be present. If the river is popular for canoeing or rafting, a locally prepared map might tell you more about the lake and its river than you can find elsewhere.

Some bigger lakes have been surveyed separately from the surrounding land, so you should be able to get official charts. However, you might find that navigational aids in the water and on shore don't follow standard patterns. The symbols could be peculiar to that chart.

Some reservoirs can be regarded as large lakes. Since they are man-made, you are more likely to find navigational helps and prepared maps. You might find that the only map is posted at an access point, and you will have to copy the information you need. The dam might be quite massive. It certainly gives you a navigational focus from which to work.

Tidal Waters

Conditions at sea are very different from those on inland waters or on shore, so a *nautical chart* is very different from a map of a land area. Its use is similar once you understand the symbols and features, but you have to make much more use of a compass.

Most charts are printed on heavy, water-resistant paper. They are not folded like land maps. A large one might have a fold across it center, but otherwise charts are kept flat or rolled so that they can be laid out flat with a smooth surface for accurately marking courses on them. The margin contains plenty of information, but you must refer to a separate sheet for a legend because the many symbols and other details you need to know will not fit in the usual margin. Instead of just a north indication in the margin, a complete compass rose is printed on the chart itself. It might be repeated elsewhere on a large chart. This rose shows north and a circle of degrees (possibly marked every two degrees) from true north. Inside, another marked circle is based on magnetic north.

The scale of a chart will be in a *nautical miles* (6080 feet) or in feet (for a large-scale harbor plan). A metric scale might also be included. American charts are produced by the National Ocean Survey. Those charts for ocean voyages are drawn to small scales, but for navigating close to the shore (called *pilotage*), charts have large scales so that ample details can be shown. For large bays or river estuaries popular with pleasure craft, large-scale charts of suitable size are bound in book form.

Charts of waters close to shore are likely to be of most interest to you. You will find that the coastline is shown, but not much behind it except landmarks that can be seen from the sea. Roads might be noted, if traffic on them can be seen from a boat. High land would be indicated, possibly with a picture showing how it looks from the sea. If you need shore information, you must have a land map as well. In any case, comparing a chart with a map of the same area to see the way common features are portrayed can be interesting.

Tides must be considered by boaters and chart makers. If the rise and fall is only a few feet, you might be able to ignore the tidal effect, but in many places it is considerably more. The record tide in the Bay of Fundy, northwest of Nova Scotia, is near 80 feet! As well as rising and falling, the water moves back and forth, so a wise boater makes use of tidal streams. A rising tide is called a *flood* tide. A falling tide is an *ebb* tide. In most places, *high* and *low water* are just over 6 hours apart.

Tides rise higher and drop lower near the full and new moon. These tides are called *spring* tides. Those with the smallest range, midway between the full and new moon, are called *neap* tides. You will find tide times and details in *tide tables*, which you can locally, or in the large *Nautical Almanac*, published annually by the National Ocean Survey.

Where land is exposed at low water and covered at high water, the chart has indications of sand, rock, mud, or other type of ground, and how far it extends. A shallow foreshore might dry out for a mile offshore, and you need to know this information. Sandbanks in a channel might also dry out.

Depths are shown with contour lines (FIG. 13-4A), with a figure on each line. You will have to check in the margin what this figure represents—it could be feet, meters, or fathoms. Farther from shore, depths can vary in a way that is not suitable for linking with contour, or sounding, lines, so spot depths are indicated (FIG. 13-4B). If you are entering an estuary in a deep-draft craft, you need to know about depths.

Electronic devices, such as *echo sounders*, are available for measuring depths, but without one, you can use the traditional method of lowering a weighted line, or *lead line*, over the side and checking how much of the line is immersed. You can read in the Bible (Acts of the Apostles, chapter 27) about St. Paul's shipwreck. The sailors sounded this way and found that the water was getting shallower and that they were being washed ashore. In more recent times, boaters had a traditional way of calling depths. Two fathoms was "by the mark twain"—that's how the famous American author chose his name.

Lighthouses are well-known signals for mariners, but many smaller marks are also used, particularly near harbor entrances and in large estuaries. Buoys of distinctive shapes, and some with tops marks, indicate dangers or sides of channels. Most buoys carry lights with special flashing

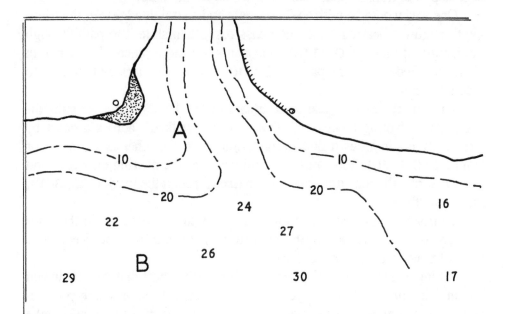

Fig. 13-4. *A nautical chart shows contour depths and spot depths.*

sequences. Buoys might have a large number painted on them. All are marked on the chart, with their details, so that navigator can identify them.

Taking Bearings on Board

When boating close to shore or entering a harbor or estuary, much navigation is done by identifying buoys or shore marks and setting course to suit. In poor visibility, you might have to go from buoy to buoy, using a compass.

In a boat, you cannot set your chart in relation to objects you can identify. The boat will be steered by a compass mounted permanently in a *binnacle*, or stand, in front of the helm. It is a floating card type with *gimbals* to keep it level when the boat rocks. The helmsman steers by keeping the required bearing opposite the lubber line. In most craft, you cannot use that compass for taking sights. You often have to get bearings quickly because the boat tosses, so you need a bearing or sighting compass. You might manage with a simple compass, but with a bearing compass, you can drop your eye as soon as you have secured the sight and read the bearing.

The large compass roses on the chart are there for you to use instead of the protractor you might use on a land map. Suppose you have identified a mark on shore and on the chart and read its bearing with a compass. The next step is to transfer that bearing to a line on the map.

One way would be with a 90° triangle and a straightedge. Set the triangle through the bearing on the compass rose, then slide it to pass through the identified mark (FIG. 13-5A). You can get a large piece of transparent plastic marked with many parallel lines to put over the mark and the rose to read a bearing (FIG. 13-5B).

The expert way is to use *parallel rules* (FIG. 13-5C), a pair of straightedges with pivoting metal arms that can be "walked" across a chart by alternately holding down one straightedge while the other is swung to or from it (FIG. 13-5D). You can set the rule edge to the bearing on a rose and move it across the map until one edge passes through the mark (FIG. 13-5E), then draw the line.

Charts have good surfaces for marking with soft pencils, so the lines are easy to erase. Sharpen your pencil frequently for a fine line. Keep pens or hard pencils away from a chart.

Taking one bearing will give you a line on the chart that you know you are on. That line might be all you want, but to find the spot where you are, you must take another cross bearing. If you can identify two marks, take

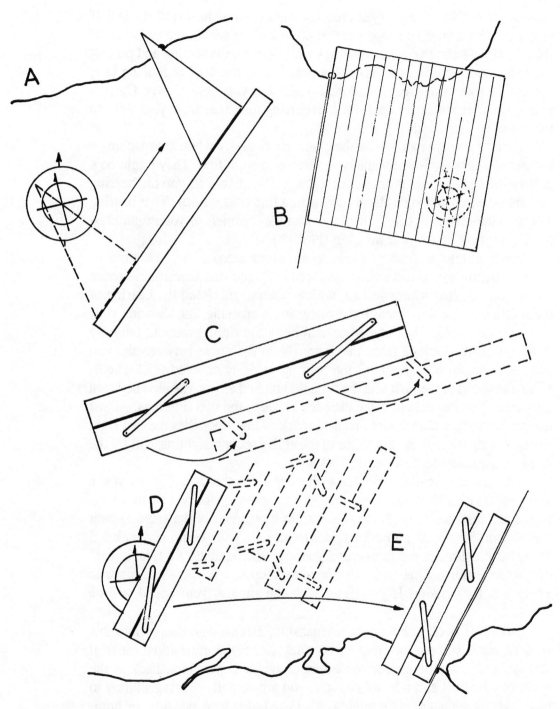

Fig. 13-5. *You can transfer bearings to and from a compass rose on a chart with a triangle, a ruled sheet of plastic, or parallel rules.*

bearings of both so that you get crossing lines on the chart (FIG. 13-6A). If possible, take a third bearing; your position will be within the cocked hat. (FIG. 13-6B). Getting accurate readings while the boat is tossing and putting the results on the chart quickly takes practice. If the boat is moving fast, you can be some way from the plotted position if you work slowly. Carry a pair of dividers with your chart for transferring distances from your lines to the scale, or vice versa.

Transits might be shown on the chart, particularly when approaching a harbor. Transits are features that you want to keep in line. They might be a radio mast and a nearer prominent building. The chart tells you the bearing you are on when you sight these objects in a line (FIG. 13-6C). That bearing might be the course to take to lead you into the channel, or you might need a cross bearing to get your position (FIG. 13-6D).

You might not find many marks to use along a coast. If you are traveling at a steady speed and course and can only see one identifiable shore mark, you can find where you are with a *running fix*. Read the bearing of the mark. Draw a line through the mark and a crossing line showing your course (FIG. 13-6E). The course line will be in the right direction, but only at an estimated distance from the shore. Note the angle between the two lines. Continue on course until the bearing angle is doubled (FIG. 13-6F). From the speed of the boat and the time that passed as you traveled between the points, you can calculate the distance between the two sightings. Adjust the position of the course line distance mark so that it touches the two sight lines. The distance from the shore mark at the second sighting will be the same as the distance traveled (FIG. 13-6G).

This method, called "doubling the angle on the bow," gives you a good rough check on position, but an unknown quantity can interfere. Speed and distance through the water are not necessarily the same as over the bottom. You must allow for tidal streams. If your boat only makes 5 *knots* (nautical miles per hour), and you are moving against a tidal stream of 5 knots, your engine will work hard to keep you in the same place in relation to the bottom. If you travel with the stream, your speed will be doubled.

Since this book is not about seamanship, I cannot go deeply into this subject, but if you are traveling far on tidal water, you must allow for tidal streams and, sometimes, for the effect of wind. If you look back at the wake of your boat and it is not straight, you are actually drifting slightly to one side rather than going straight (FIG. 13-7A), due to wind, tide, or both.

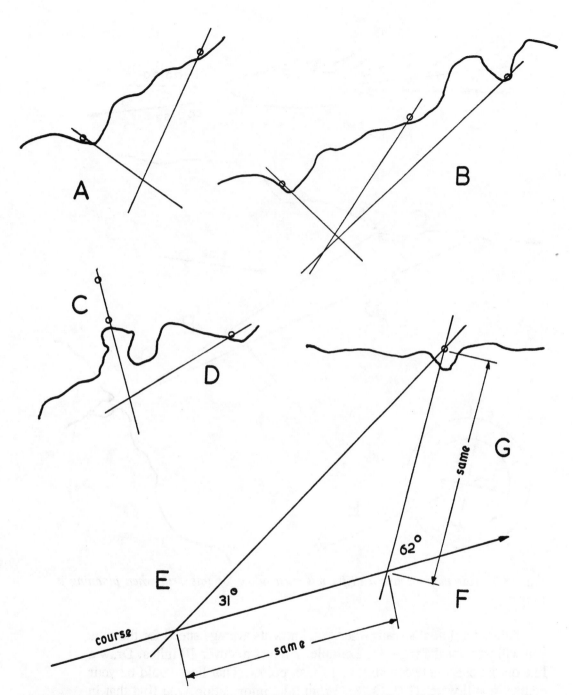

Fig. 13-6. *Near the coast, bearings give you positions (A, B, C, and D). If you see only one landmark, you can take a running fix (E, F, and G).*

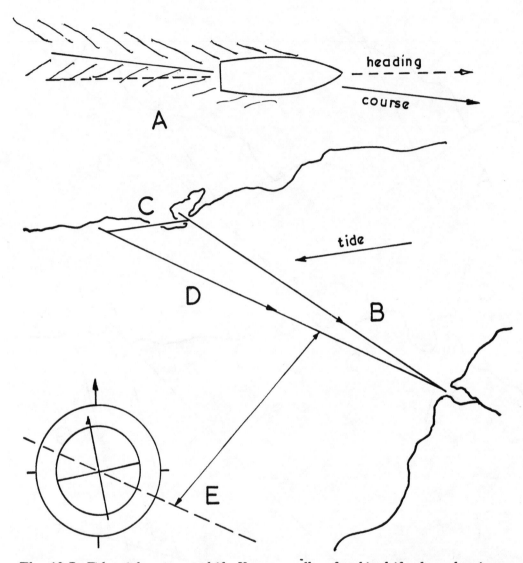

Fig. 13-7. *Tide might cause a drift. You must allow for this drift when planning a course.*

Allow for a tidal stream when you know its average speed for the time you will take for the trip—for example, 2 hours to cover 10 miles. Draw a line on the chart between start and finish points. That line would be your course in still water (FIG. 13-7B). From tidal information, you find that in two hours the tidal stream might push your boat off course 3 miles. Draw a line through the starting point in the direction of the tidal stream to a scale length of 3 miles (FIG. 13-7C). Complete the triangle. That line is the course you must steer to allow for the tide (FIG. 13-7D). To find the compass setting, use your parallel rules or other means to transfer the line to the compass rose (FIG. 13-7E).

In this case, your boat heading will be to one side of the direction you are going. In an extreme case, with a strong tidal flow, you might be heading almost into the stream, doing what a kayaker calls a "ferry glide." Because tidal streams change direction after about 6 hours and are strongest during the middle of the 6 hours, you meet complications in planning a long journey, particularly in a slow-moving boat.

Compasswork with a map ashore or a chart afloat involve many of the same principles. Learning about one helps you with the other. Tidal waters present you with many problems different from those you experience elsewhere. This chapter offers only introductory notes. If you are interested in the fascinating experience of using any sort of craft, read books on seamanship and take lessons before you go afloat.

14

Maintaining Your Equipment

MAPS AND COMPASSES ARE FAIRLY STRONG, BUT YOU MUST TAKE care of them. Even if a map is not valuable in cash terms, its loss or damage during an expedition cannot be measured in dollars. Compasses and other equipment should not suffer in normal use. Steel and brass might corrode during damp storage. Some plastics become brittle if they get too cold.

Map Folding

A map can be supplied flat, rolled, or folded in various ways. If you want to fold your own map, consider the size of any case into which it must fit. Also consider how you want to examine it in the field. Fully opening a large map during rain or a high wind would be a nuisance. A small map folded back with the working surface outside will have everything you want visible. If you fold it again, you still can find easily the details you want (FIG. 14-1A).

If the folded map still would be too big with those folds, you can have everything available to see without opening very much at one time if you fold it in a zigzag or accordian manner. Fold the map back on itself in half lengthwise (FIG. 14-1B). Divide it horizontally into sections of convenient width—about 5 inches probably would do (FIG. 14-1C). Fold these section divisions alternate ways (FIG. 14-1D). Rub down all the folds with a rounded piece of wood or a smooth knife handle (FIG. 14-1E). Now fold the whole

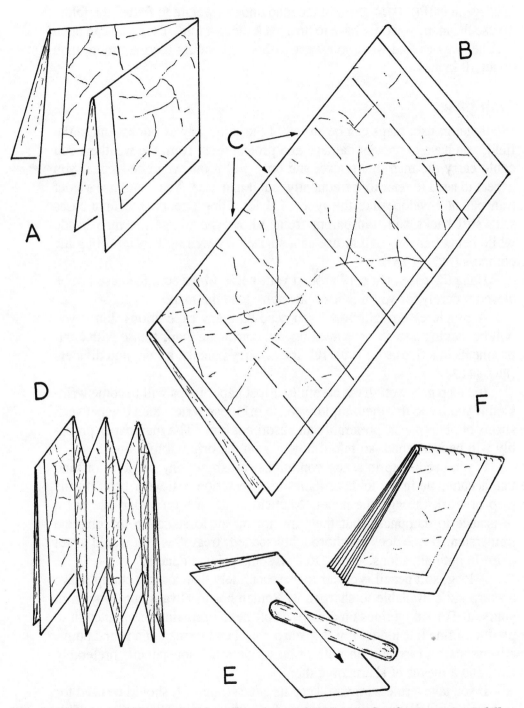

Fig. 14-1. *You can fold a map so that you can see what you need without opening it fully.*

package in half (FIG. 14-1F). Put the map under a weight to flatten the folds. To use the map, you only have to turn back the last fold. Then you can open it either way to find what you want without spreading the map more than about 10 inches.

Map Cases

When not in use, maps can be stored in the same way as books, but in the field, you have to prevent damage and protect them from the weather. You could carry the map in a pocket and only pull it out when needed. If you expect to need to refer to it frequently, put it in a case. You could use a stout transparent envelope like the type used for filing papers, but map cases with stiff backs and transparent fronts allow you to see the map inside while being hard enough to use as a surface for writing or supporting the compass (FIG. 14-2A).

Hang the case on a cord around your neck. Make sure the case can be closed securely, or you might accidentally lose the map.

A simple case might be all you need on many expeditions, but if you will be making a survey or checking and marking a map, a case with compartments in a flap cover is useful. It can carry pencils, a rule, and dividers (FIG. 14-2B).

If a map gets wet, dry it carefully. Most paper maps will become wrinkled if you try to dry them rapidly. Wipe off loose water, then dry between sheets of plain paper, preferably an absorbent type. The map paper probably will be weakened, so refold it gently on the original fold lines.

If you use a map in sandy conditions, brush out any particles of sand that accumulate in the folds or their abrasive action will wear print off the map or work through the paper. Nautical charts are on paper that has a resistance to dampness, but they are not meant to stand up to complete immersion. If one does get thoroughly soaked, treat it as you would a wet map. In both situations, expect to lose some printed details.

A long, soft pencil is easier to use accurately than a short stump. Have a sharp knife available to sharpen it. Remember to always cut away from yourself. For ruling lines on a map, a soft pencil remains sharp enough to produce a fine line longer if it is given a chisel end instead of a round point. Always start an expedition with at least one good soft pencil, preferably two, and a means of sharpening them.

If you take a rule with you, keep its edge straight. It should be used for measuring and drawing lines only, not for cutting against with a knife. This action might gouge out the thin edge.

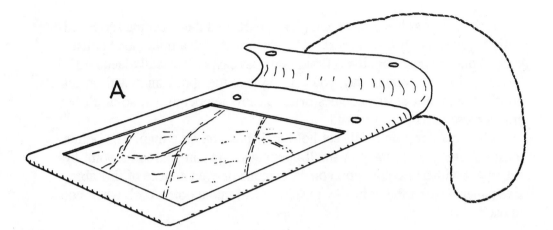

A

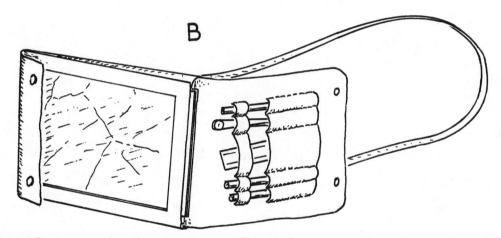

B

Fig. 14-2. *A map is best kept in a case, with or without compartments for pencils and instruments.*

Compasses

Most compasses do not need any special storage, but do keep them face up. When you are traveling, do not carry the compass in your hand or loose in a pocket. Have it on a cord around your neck or secured to a buttonhole, then tucked in a pocket or inside your shirt.

Your compass will almost certainly be liquid-filled. If an air bubble appears, it will not affect performance. If much air gets into the case, the damping of motion will be less and the needle will gyrate more before it settles. Don't attempt to refill a compass yourself. If it needs attention, return it to the makers for repair.

If the compass has transparent plastic parts and they become scratched or dull, you can improve the surface by rubbing it with a mild metal polish, such as one intended for silver. Brass compass cases are usually lacquered, but if the lacquer wears away, you can improve the appearance with metal polish. Some thin brass becomes brittle at low temperatures, so don't let any of these parts get very cold.

Blunt divider points will not hold their position on a map. The points must be level for accuracy at small openings. You can sharpen a point by rubbing it with a circular action on an oilstone or even a piece of fine abrasive paper. Protect the points by pushing them into a bottle cork when not in use.

Appendix
Measurements

1 statute mile = 1760 yards = 5280 feet
1 nautical mile = 2026.8 yards = 6080 feet
1 fathom = 6 feet
Knots are nautical miles per hour
(quote speed as X knots, not X knots per hour)

Metric Measures of Length

10 millimeters (mm) = 1 centimeter (cm) = about 0.394 inches
100 centimeters (cm) = 1 meter (m) = about 39.37 inches
1000 meters (m) = 1 kilometer (km) = about 0.62 mile
8 kilometers = about 5 miles

Glossary

acute—Describes an angle less than 90°.

aerial survey—Survey based on photographs taken from the air.

aiming off—Plotting a course to one side of the final destination to make use of a feature that will lead into it, in case of error.

alidade—A sighting device used in surveying that consists of sights arranged over a straightedge.

Antarctic Circle—Line of latitude 66^1/$_2$° south of the equator.

Arctic Circle—Line of latitude 66^1/$_2$° north of the equator.

area survey—A method of surveying that uses triangles to pinpoint the location of objects to be mapped.

atlas—A book of maps.

bearing—The direction of one point from another as determined with a compass.

bearing compass—A compass that has sights so that the compass bearing can be read while the object is sighted.

bezel—The rim of a watch or compass.

binnacle—The stand or case for a compass used in steering a ship, usually containing gimbals to keep the compass level.

boundary—Limit or dividing line shown on a map, usually imaginary and not marked on the ground.

buoy—A float used to mark channels, shallows, or an object under the surface of the water.

card—The disc of a compass, marked in degrees, especially the type that revolves with the needle.

cardinal points—North (N), south (S), east (E), and west (W) on a compass.

cartography—Science and art of making maps.

celestial navigation—Finding one's way by using the stars and sun, particularly when traveling on the ocean.

chart—Map intended for navigation at sea or in the air.

cocked hat—The triangle of crossed lines that might occur in plotting three bearings that do not meet exactly.

compass rose—Drawn compass circle marked in degrees, particularly on a chart.

contour—A line on a map passing through points of the same elevation.

control—A point that must be visited in an orienteering competition.

coordinates—Lines of identification on a map, such as latitude and longitude.

daymark—A buoy that is not lit at night.

dead reckoning—Working out one's progress from distance, time, and direction only.

declination—The angular difference between true and magnetic north at a particular point.

deviation—Compass error on a particular heading.

draft—The depth of water a ship needs to float in.

drift—The tendency to move off course due to water or wind at sea.

echo sounder—Electronic device for measuring depths from a boat.

elevation—Vertical distance of a point above a datum; usually in feet above sea level on a map.

estuary—The mouth of a river into which sea water can flow.

fathom—A unit of length equal to 6 feet, used to measure depth of water.

fix—To obtain a position on a map or chart as a result of taking bearings.

gazetteer—List or index of places on a map, usually with grid references.

gimbals—Pivoted rings used to support a compass so that it remains level when a ship pitches and rolls.

gradient—The rate of ascent or descent of a hill; a measure of steepness.

grid—System of lines crossing a map, used for references.

grid reference—A numbered location using the margin numbering of grid lines across a map.

handrail—A physical feature used as a guide in orienteering.

hatching—Lines drawn on a map as shading to indicate slopes.

high water—The highest level reached by a tide.

index contour—A thick contour line marked with a number that indicates elevation above sea level.

International Date Line—The meridian of longitude 180° from the prime meridian.

knot—Nautical mile per hour.

landmark—Man-made or natural feature that can be used to determine a location or bearing.

large-scale map—A map that shows a small part of the earth's surface in great detail.

latitude—Angular distance of a point north or south of the equator.

layer tinting—Coloring a map between contour lines to emphasize differences in elevation.

lead line—Weighted line used for sounding the depth of water.

leeway—Off-course sideways movement of a boat through the water.

legend—An explanation of symbols on a map.

line survey—A method of surveying that uses lines of known positions and length.

lodestone—Naturally magnetic iron ore, once used to make compasses.

longitude—Angular distance of a point east or west of the prime meridian.

low water—The lowest level reached by a tide.

lubber line—A mark on a compass bowl rim, particularly on a ship's steering compass, indicating the heading.

magnetic north—The pole to which a compass points.

margin—The open space around a map that usually contains the scale, north point, legend, and other information.

meridian—Great circle on the surface of the earth that passes through both the poles. All points on it have the same longitude.

nautical mile—1 minute of latitude (6080 feet).

neatline—Border line between a map and its margin.

obtuse—Describes an angle greater than 90°.

offset course—A route that leads to one side of the eventual destination to make use of a feature that leads to the destination.

orienteering—A sport that combines map and compass skills with cross-country running.

orienting a map—Establishing the correct relationship among the map, compass, and ground.

parallel of latitude—A line connecting all points in a circle the same distance and direction from the equator.

parallel rules—An instrument consisting of linked straightedges used to transfer bearings between the compass rose on a chart and the point concerned.

physical map—A map that concentrates on natural features.

pilotage—Navigation at sea within visual or radio contact of the shore.

plan—A very large-scale map of a small area, such as a town.

plane table—A supported drawing board used with an alidade or compass for making a survey.

plot—To mark on the map the results of sights and bearings.

political map—A map that concentrates on man-made features such as towns, roads, and boundaries.

prime meridian—Line of longitude universally recognized as 0°. It runs through Greenwich, England.

protractor—Instrument used for measuring degrees.

quadrangle—Four-sided area bounded by meridians of longitude and parallels of latitude.

quadrangle map—Geological survey map based on a quadrangle, described in degrees or minutes.

reciprocal bearing—Direction 180° opposite the original bearing.

relief—Heights and hollows of the land or sea bed.

relief shading—Emphasizing relief on a map by adding shadow effects.

representative fraction—The scale of a map expressed as a fraction relating distance on the map with distance on the ground.

road map—Any map mainly concerned with roads and the places they join, intended for use by motorists.

roamer—Device for measuring intermediate distances in a grid system.

running fix—A method of determining location at sea using only one landmark.

scale—Relationship between a distance on a map and the distance it represents on the surface of the earth.

scale rule—A rule marked to suit the scale of a map.

setting a map—Arranging a map in the same direction as the part of the earth's surface it represents.

sighting compass—A bearing compass. The bearing can be read at the same time the sight is taken.

sketch map—A freehand map drawn as a rough guide or as a preliminary step to a survey.

small-scale map—A map that shows a large part of the earth's surface with little detail.

sounding—Finding the depth of water at a particular point.

spot elevation—Point on a map where the actual height is shown.

survey—System of collecting information that will be used in making a map.

symbols—Conventional signs on a map used to indicate features on the surface of the earth.

template (templet)—Alternate name for a roamer.

terrain—The physical features of a tract of land.

thwart—A rower's seat that extends across a boat.

tide—Periodic movement of water at sea, involving horizontal movement as well as rise and fall. An **ebbtide** is a falling tide. A **flood tide** is a rising tide. A **neap tide** occurs midway between the full and new moon, when the level of water changes the least amount. A **spring tide** occurs during a full moon or a new moon, when the water rises to its highest point and drops to its lowest point.

tide table—A chart that lists the times and details of local tides.

topographic map—Map representing the vertical as well as the horizontal positions of the features shown.

transit—Getting two landmarks in line to establish your position line.

traverse—A line surveyed across a plot of land; to make a survey using such lines.

triangulation—A method of surveying by taking bearings and distances in the form of triangles.

Tropic of Cancer—Parallel of latitude $23^1/_2\,°$N.

Tropic of Capricorn—Parallel of latitude $23^1/_2\,°$S.

Index

flood tides, 128
folding maps, 136-138

G

gazetteer, 3
gimbals, compass stabilizers, 130
globes, 47
gradients, 7, 17-19
   road maps, 53-54
grids and grid references, location finding, 48-50

H

handrails, orienteering, 93
hatching, 15
height estimation, landmarks, 98-100
height of land (*see* elevation)

I

index contours, 17
International Date Line, 45-46
International Orienteering Federation (IOF), 85

K

knots, 132, 141

L

lake navigation, 126-127
landmarks
   setting maps, 37-38
   symbols, 9-10
   wilderness hiking, 81-82
large-scale maps, 2, 10-11
latitude, 3, 44-47
layer tinting, contour lines, 19
lead lines, depth of water, 129
legends, 2-3
lighthouses, 129
line surveys, drawing maps, 104-107
location finding, 44-50
   grids and grid references, 48-50

latitude, 3, 44-47
   longitude, 3, 44-47
lodestones, 23
longitude, 3, 44-47
lost, finding your way out, 83-84
lubber lines, compasses, 27

M

magnetic north, 30-31
margins, 2-3
measuring distance, 11, 50, 97-98
measuring speed in knots, 132
measuring width of waterways, 100-102
meridians of longitude (*see also* longitude), 45-46
metric measurements, conversions, 141
miles vs. nautical miles, 11, 128, 141

N

Nautical Almanac, 128
nautical charts (*see also* waterways), 127-130
nautical miles, 11, 128, 141
neap tides, 128
neatlines, 2
north vs. magnetic north, 30-31
nun buoys, 124

O

obstructions, wilderness hiking, 79-81
offset bearings, wilderness hiking, 70, 82-83
orienteering, 85-94
   clothing, 90
   compass selection, 86-87
   controls or check points, 87
   distance and speed orienteering, 90-91
   equipment, 88-90
   events, typical sequence, 91-94

handrails, 93
International Orienteering Federation (IOF), 85
map selection, 87-88
night orienteering events, 94
relay events, 94
scales, 87-88
score events, 93
symbols on maps, 88-89
orienting maps (*see* setting maps)

P

parallel rules, 130-132
parallels of latitude (*see also* latitude), 45-46
physical maps, 2
pilotage, 128
plane table surveying, 114-118
plans, 2
plotting, 40
political maps, 2
prime meridian, 45-46
projections, 47
protractors, 30
   setting maps, 40-41

Q

quadrangle maps (*see* topographic maps)

R

railroad symbols, 8
reciprocal bearings, 65, 67
relay events, orienteering, 94
relief shading, 15
representative fraction, scale, 1, 10
rivers (*see* waterway navigation)
road maps, 51-61
   elevation, 53-54
   gradients, 53-54
   numbering and identification symbols, 54-56
   road surveys, 109-111
   route planning, difficult routes, 59-60